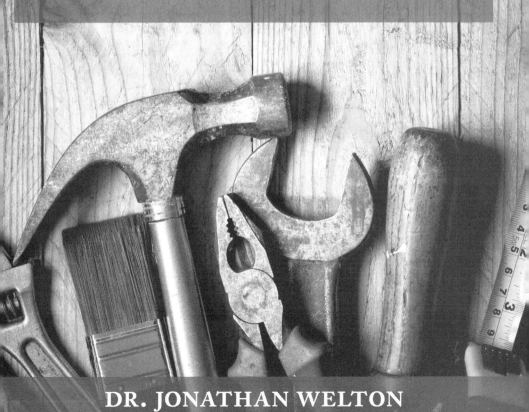

MW00696537

FOREWORD

EQUIPPING THE EQUIPPERS

The Handbook for raising up Apostles, Prophets, Evangelists, Pastors and Teachers

DR. JONATHAN WELTON

Equipping the Equippers
The Handbook for raising up Apostles, Prophets, Evangelists, Pastors, and Teachers.
Dr. Jonathan Welton, Copyright © 2017

First printing June 2017, 3000, Second printing September 2017, 2000

All rights reserved. This book is protected by the copyright laws of the United States of America. This book may not be copied or reprinted for commercial gain or profit. The use of short quotations or occasional page copying for personal or group study is permitted and encouraged. Permission will be granted upon request.

Unless otherwise identified, Scripture quotations are taken from the THE HOLY BIBLE, NEW INTERNATIONAL VERSION®, NIV®. Copyright © 1973, 1978, 1984, 2010 by Biblica, Inc.™ www.xulonpress.com. Scripture quotations marked KJV are taken from the King James Version. Scripture quotations marked NKJV are taken from the New King James Version. Copyright © 1982 by Thomas Nelson, Inc. Used by permission. All rights reserved. Scripture quotations marked NIV are taken from the HOLY BIBLE, NEW INTERNATIONAL VERSION®, Copyright © 1973, 1978, 1984 International Bible Society. Used by permission of Zondervan. All rights reserved. Emphasis within Scripture quotations is the author's own.

Welton Academy
P.O. Box 92126
Rochester, NY 14692
www.weltonacademy.com

Printed in the United States
ISBN: 978-0-9981761-2-3

OTHER TITLES BY DR. WELTON

The School of the Seers

Normal Christianity

Eyes of Honor

Raptureless

Understanding the Seven Churches of Revelation

The Art of Revelation

Understanding the Whole Bible

New Age Masquerade

The Advancing Kingdom

New Covenant Revolution

CONTENTS

FOREWORD

By Danny Silk

In his letter to the Ephesians, Paul stated that Jesus has given His church a set of "gifts"—apostles, prophets, evangelists, pastors, and teachers—to equip the people of God to fulfill their purpose and mission in the earth, ultimately glorifying Him through love, maturity, and unity (Eph. 4:11-16).

The teachings and opinions on the subject of the "fivefold ministry" are both extensive and convoluted. Many of them have been wonderful, unifying contributions to the body of Christ, while others have repeatedly been used as divisive tools that generate fear, frustration, and control. These misuses have led to extremes such as rejecting the validity of modern-day apostles and prophets, or constructing oppressive hierarchies that over-empower particular individuals in religious networks or organizations. It is vital that we sort out the misunderstandings, confusion, and misapplications of these gifts to the church and restore them to their proper place and function in church government. Without these gifts, the saints will not be properly equipped.

We who are leaders in the body of Christ need some serious adjustments in the way we think about the purpose and structure of government in the church. First, we must return to the ultimate purpose Jesus revealed in the prayer He taught us to pray: "Your kingdom come. Your will be done on earth as it is in heaven" (Matt. 6:10). Our role as leaders is to equip the body of Christ—not to give money, build great programs, and live morally upright lives—but to make earth look more and more like heaven.

Next, we need to realign our governmental structure with the Scriptural designation of who comes "first." Paul wrote: "And God has appointed these in the church: first apostles, second prophets, third teachers, after that workers of miracles, then gifts of healings, helps, administrations, varieties of tongues" (1 Cor. 12:28). Throughout most of the church today, we have determined that we will have "first" pastors and teachers, then administrative leaders and evangelists. Our set of priorities flies in the face of what "God has appointed in the church." We carry both an ignorance and arrogance that somehow the five gifts of Christ are no longer applicable or useful, and that we can narrow our leadership roles down to the three we think we can use as we build the church. This works to a certain degree as we spread the gospel around the world. All it costs us is heaven.

In short, Jesus taught us to prioritize heaven on earth, and to build a leadership structure that would work as a receptacle for heaven on earth. I don't know where we lost this focus and understanding, but I am excited to see it being reestablished all over the world today. It amazes me that Jesus would trust us with such valuable opportunities and resources at this place in time and history. There is no greater privilege than to be trusted by Christ with His Spirit and His Bride, and to co-labor with Him to establish His kingdom in the earth.

Equipping the Equippers is a book for our time, and is right on time. Dr. Jonathan Welton takes us on a Scriptural journey through the functions of each of these five gifts of Christ and how they work together, and shows us how to apply the useful structure in the modern-day church. He is deeply thorough and clear in presenting a teaching that I hope leads to paradigm shifts throughout the body of Christ. Whether you are considering a fresh perspective on the subject or looking for ammunition to further your case, this is an excellent book.

Danny Silk
President of Loving On Purpose
Author of *Culture of Honor* and *Keep Your Love On*

INTRODUCTION

The green military jeep came to a screeching halt in the mud outside a soggy tent. The general's boots splashed as he stepped from the jeep into the darkness. He entered the tent to find five officers standing around a large map stretched across a table. The officers snapped to attention.

The general wasted no time. "Tell me what is going on here!" he ordered. "Headquarters keeps getting reports that you have a brutally high level of casualties and your units are dysfunctional!"

One of the weary officers exchanged glances with the men and women standing near him. He coughed and then looked back at the general: "Do we have permission to speak freely, sir?"

"Permission granted," the general answered, his face a mask of sternness.

"Well sir, honestly . . . we were not equipped for this. We were taught to be shepherds. We can fix marriages, help raise godly children, and teach people how to live healthy Christian lives, but we weren't built for frontline warfare. I don't even know what I am doing here! I am constantly asked to do things that are beyond my training and capacity. I am shell-shocked and living on the edge of burnout."

The general's expression softened. He scanned the faces of the officers standing before him. In a less harsh voice, he asked, "Does this represent what is happening here?"

They nodded sheepishly and one said, "More or less."

The general clasped his hands behind his back. "Where are the prophets who are meant to be in this unit to regularly bring communication from headquarters and encourage you to keep pushing forward?"

The officers looked at each other for a long moment. A woman finally spoke, "We typically have a roving prophet visit us once a year—sometimes less."

The general asked, "And the teachers who are meant to bring fresh bread and cutting-edge strategies for advancing the kingdom?"

Another officer answered, "We sometimes read their books—if we can find the time . . ." His voice trailed off, and he stared down toward the battle map.

"And the evangelists?" said the general. "Please tell me that you have some of those to rescue the captives and bring in new soldiers?"

"Evangelists? Not really. Most of our people are afraid of the darkness. We get together and sing, take offerings, listen to familiar messages, and hope reinforcements will come."

The general gave a resigned nod. "And I'm guessing you have no apostles either. Am I right?"

A woman nodded. "Correct, sir. You are the first we have seen in decades."

The general leaned forward. "Do you know what an apostle does?"

"No sir, not really."

"Well, ultimately, I am here to serve you so that you can best serve the kingdom. To implement my advice, you will need to make some dramatic adjustments, but you will end up better for it." He looked each officer in the eye in turn. "I will bring in my team, which consists of five types

of leaders. We will raise up prophets from within your unit who can communicate direction from headquarters and speak life and courage into your people. I will train teachers, who will feed your people and make them strong and healthy. I will build evangelists, who will push everyone out of their foxholes and on to the battlefield to advance the kingdom."

As the general spoke, the officers' stance slowly changed from weary to invigorated. In unison, they said, "Yes, sir!"

The general nodded. "By the time I am done here, the shepherd casualty rate will have dropped dramatically, and you will have the strongest and most well-rounded soldiers available in the kingdom. It will take a major overhaul, but we can get back to the original blueprint and set up your outpost correctly. Thank you for allowing me to bring these adjustments to you. It is my pleasure to serve you. Let's begin."

The officers breathed a collective sigh of relief. They had been waiting decades for new apostles to appear. The last wave of apostles had flunked out of basic training when they tried to control people rather than humbly serving them. For years, rumors had circulated that a new batch of apostles had actually been released into the battlefront. Now they had finally arrived, and together, they could begin to advance the kingdom.

OUR CURRENT PROBLEM

Modern Christianity has struggled with the reality that God is releasing apostles in the current church system. Yet this is not a new problem. I believe that every generation has struggled with this same problem, because the apostolic grace is unique, and it creates challenges for current systems, which may have become more cozy than effective. For the sake of time, I will not be reviewing how every generation of church history has responded to the new apostles God has released, but I do want to look at how the very first generation of apostles encountered this exact challenge:

In those days Peter stood up among the believers (a group numbering about a hundred and twenty) and said, "Brothers and sisters, the Scripture had to be fulfilled in which the Holy Spirit spoke long ago through David concerning Judas, who served as guide for those who arrested Jesus. He was one of our number and shared in our ministry."

(With the payment he received for his wickedness, Judas bought a field; there he fell headlong, his body burst open and all his intestines spilled out. Everyone in Jerusalem heard about this, so they called that field in their language Akeldama, that is, Field of Blood.)

"For," said Peter, "it is written in the Book of Psalms: 'May his place be deserted; let there be no one to dwell in it,' and, 'May another take his place of leadership.'

"Therefore it is necessary to choose one of the men who have been with us the whole time the Lord Jesus was living among us, beginning from John's baptism to the time when Jesus was taken up from us. For one of these must become a witness with us of his resurrection."

So they nominated two men: Joseph called Barsabbas (also known as Justus) and Matthias. Then they prayed, "Lord, you know everyone's heart. Show us which of these two you have chosen to take over this apostolic ministry, which Judas left to go where he belongs." Then they cast lots, and the lot fell to Matthias; so he was added to the eleven apostles. (Acts 1:15-26)

Peter quoted from two proof texts in Psalms to show that Judas' death was predicted and that he should be replaced. Notice that the eleven apostles had two qualified candidates in front of them, yet from their perspective they only needed one, because they were simply trying to get back to the number twelve. Later in Acts, the number ends up at eleven again because of the death of the first apostle, James:

It was about this time that King Herod arrested some who belonged to the church, intending to persecute them. He had James, the brother of John, put to death with the sword. When he saw that this met with approval among the Jews, he proceeded to seize Peter also. This happened during the Festival of Unleavened Bread. (Acts 12:1-3)

When James was put to death, the other eleven did not reconvene to replace him and return to twelve apostles. Peter did not stand up again and quote from Psalms, and no one predicted that James would be martyred. I believe that what we see in the original group of apostles, which I refer to as the Jerusalem apostles, is a system that would have died out. After replacing Judas, the group had no plan for implementing new apostles. Even in Acts 1, when they had two qualified candidates, they only chose one! Eventually, all twelve apostles would have been martyred without having raised up new ones. But the Holy Spirit had a different plan.

Over in Antioch, the Holy Spirit began to speak through the prophets and teachers about raising up two new apostles. This not only replaced the martyred James; it actually moved the number of overall apostles to thirteen:

Now in the church at Antioch there were prophets and teachers: Barnabas, Simeon called Niger, Lucius of Cyrene, Manaen (who had been brought up with Herod the tetrarch) and Saul. While they were worshiping the Lord and fasting, the Holy Spirit said, "Set apart for me Barnabas and Saul for the work to which I have called them." So after they had fasted and prayed, they placed their hands on them and sent them off. (Acts 13:1-3)

The original model is straightforward: apostles create apostles. Jesus, "our apostle" (Heb. 3:1) created the twelve (Luke 6:1-3), and the eleven raised up Matthias (Acts 1:26). Yet the Jerusalem apostles weren't raising up any new apostles. Therefore, the Holy Spirit went to the prophets and teachers in Antioch and had them raise up the new apostles. Not only did the Holy Spirit break the barrier of the limited number of apostles by expanding it to thirteen, but these new apostles could also carry a revelation to the Gentiles, unencumbered by prejudice. We read of the new apostles, Paul and Barnabas, carrying the gospel all throughout the known world, while the Jerusalem apostles struggled with the uncircumcised receiving the gospel and were weighed down with an old perspective. These new apostles were able to carry a grace that was different from the grace the old ones carried:

> *"On the contrary, they recognized that I had been entrusted with the task of preaching the gospel to the uncircumcised, just as Peter had been to the circumcised. For God, who was at work in Peter as an apostle to the circumcised, was also at work in me as an apostle to the Gentiles."* (Gal. 2:7-8)

Nowadays, the Holy Spirit has been speaking through prophets and teachers, declaring that a new move of apostles will be released in the earth. We have been seeing some of these apostles coming forth in the last two decades, but we have also seen a lot of confusion, mistakes, and abuse. It is with this new batch of grace-dipped, kingdom officers in mind that I write this book to help equip the equippers.

CHAPTER ONE

FIVEFOLD:
A Clearer Definition

The goal of being a follower of Jesus is to be like Jesus. *"Whoever claims to live in him must live as Jesus did"* (1 John 2:6). Yet when a book is written about the fivefold ministry (apostles, prophets, evangelists, pastors, and teachers), it is easy to get lost in the weeds of church government or hierarchy. Somehow, we focus on the present reality of church politics and forget the New Testament models that have been handed down to us—even forgetting our ultimate goal of being like Jesus.

This doesn't mean we shouldn't have books about the fivefold ministry; it simply means that we need those books to remember that the purpose of five-fold ministry is, in fact, to help us become like Jesus.

Jesus Himself is an apostle: *"fix your thoughts on Jesus, whom we acknowledge as our apostle and high priest"* (Heb. 3:1b). As an apostle, Jesus replicated Himself in twelve apostles (Luke 6:12-13). None of the original foundational leaders were prophets, evangelists, pastors, or teachers; they were all apostles.

Then, on Pentecost, when the first 3,000 people accepted salvation through Jesus, we read: *"They devoted themselves to the apostles' teaching and to fellowship, to the breaking of bread and to prayer"* (Acts 2:42).

This is the foundation: Jesus the Apostle is the model, the twelve apostles were the replicas of His model, and the early church was built on the model of the twelve (Acts 2:42). Paul later writes that the church is *"built on the foundation of the apostles and prophets, with Christ Jesus himself as the chief cornerstone"* (Eph. 2:20). Everything that flowed out of the original foundation of the early church was "apostolic"—meaning "apostle-like"—in nature. New covenant prophets, evangelists, pastors, and teachers only came along later.

The apostles are not only the foundation, but also the builders: *"By the grace God has given me, **I laid a foundation as a wise builder**, and someone else is building on it. But each one should **build with care**. For no one can lay any foundation other than the one already laid, which is Jesus Christ"* (1 Cor. 3:10-11).

If we are going to build with care, as Paul admonishes the Corinthians, we must build on the foundation of Jesus (*the* Apostle) and the other apostles. So everything that the modern church does must be built on an apostolic foundation. If we continue building on the pastoral foundation that tradition has handed us, that foundation could be seriously deficient and unable to support proper structure.

Many of the other books on the fivefold ministry have focused their argument on the fact that apostles and prophets still exist in the modern church. They have debated for the right to actually call someone an apostle, and they have aimed to give a definition of what an apostle is or looks like.

My starting point is that yes, apostles do exist today, and yes, if someone is functioning as an apostle, then they should be recognized as such. We also certainly need a better definition of these gifts and how they function.[1] However, I want to move beyond arguments about the nitty-gritty of the fivefold ministry.

Here are my five goals for this book:

1. To give a clearer definition of the fivefold graces
2. To display the fivefold ministers' sphere and how each minister operates within that sphere
3. To show what the fivefold heart looks like
4. To explain how abuses and mistakes have happened in an effort to avoid repeating them
5. To demonstrate how to implement the kingdom model

At some points, I may seem to be focused exclusively on apostles, yet my larger focus is all five graces: apostles, prophets, evangelists, pastors, and teachers. However, the New Testament gives us abundant information about the apostles and comparatively little information about the other four. Also, the others were operating on the foundation of the apostles and prophets; therefore we must understand that foundation if we are to get the other ones correct.

WHAT ARE THEY FOR?

So Christ himself gave the apostles, the prophets, the evangelists, the pastors and teachers, to equip his people for works of service, so that the body of Christ may be built up until we all reach unity in the faith and in the knowledge of the Son of God and become mature, attaining to the whole measure of the fullness of Christ.

[1] If you want to read a couple of the best books on this topic which lay the foundation, I suggest:

The Complete Wineskin, Harold R. Eberle

Fivefold Ministry Made Practical, Ron Myer

Apostles Today, C. Peter Wagner

Apostles Today, Benjamin Scott

Then we will no longer be infants, tossed back and forth by the waves, and blown here and there by every wind of teaching and by the cunning and craftiness of people in their deceitful scheming. Instead, speaking the truth in love, we will grow to become in every respect the mature body of him who is the head, that is, Christ. From him the whole body, joined and held together by every supporting ligament, grows and builds itself up in love, as each part does its work. (Eph. 4:11-16)

Just as we find lists of the nine gifts of the Spirit (1 Cor. 12:1-11) and the nine fruit of the Spirit (Gal. 5:22-23), here in this passage of Ephesians, we find nine fruit of the fivefold ministry in full operation:

1. Unity: *"until we all reach unity in the faith"* (4:13).

2. Knowledge: *"and in the knowledge of the Son of God"* (4:13).

3. Maturity: *"and become mature"* (4:13).

4. Full measure of Christ: *"attaining to the whole measure of the fullness of Christ"* (4:13).

5. Not infants: *"Then we will no longer be infants"* (4:14).

6. Not falling into false teaching: *"no longer . . . tossed back and forth by the waves, and blown here and there by every wind of teaching and by the cunning and craftiness of people in their deceitful scheming"* (4:14).

7. Being a mature representation: *"Instead, speaking the truth in love, we will grow to become in every respect the mature body of him who is the head, that is, Christ"* (4:15).

8. Each part doing its work: *"as each part does its work"* (4:16).

9. The whole body built and connected in love: *"From him the whole body, joined and held together by every supporting ligament, grows and builds itself up in love"* (4:16).

At the core of these nine fruit we find common themes: unity, maturity, knowledge, right relationships, and every part being involved. This is the fruit the fivefold produces, and it is what every healthy church leader desires to see in their congregation. Why should we spend time focused on these five graces? Because they produce what the church longs to see. They are like five farmers producing five different crops, but when they are all operating, the five harvests are the ingredients that combine into the perfect "nutrition" for sustaining the church. The Christlikeness that we desire to see in the church—and that the world is waiting for from the church—cannot be grown, harvested, and produced if we lack farmers in our midst.

FOUR THINGS THEY DO

The five graces are unique and different, yet their functions in the body of Christ have at least four similarities. Let's look closer at what the fivefold practically does:

1. *They Adjust The Bones*

. . . to equip his people for works of service, so that the body of Christ may be built up until we all reach unity in the faith and in the knowledge of the Son of God and become mature, attaining to the whole measure of the fullness of Christ. (Eph. 4:12-13)

In Ephesians 4:12, the word translated "equip" is the Greek word *katartizo*, "a medical term meaning to put bones back together."[2] Just as a chiropractor aligns bones, so the fivefold equips the body of Christ by bringing its members into alignment.

[2] Alain Caron, *Apostolic Centers* (Colorado Springs, CO: Arsenal Press, 2013), 96.

Not every person is a chiropractor, and not every Christian is called to adjust the bones in the body of Christ. The body of Christ needs those who are truly graced as fivefold leaders to bring adjustments and right alignment. Many of the problems the church faces would be dealt with quickly and graciously if the fivefold ministers were all fully functioning—in other words, if the equippers were all equipped.

Here are three examples of the types of adjustments we see fivefold leaders doing in the early church:

- **They correct false doctrine:**

Among them are Hymenaeus and Alexander, whom I have handed over to Satan to be taught not to blaspheme. (1 Tim.1:20)

Their teaching will spread like gangrene. Among them are Hymenaeus and Philetus. (2 Tim. 2:17)

- **They correct false actions, such as Peter being a hypocrite:**

When Cephas came to Antioch, I opposed him to his face, because he stood condemned. For before certain men came from James, he used to eat with the Gentiles. But when they arrived, he began to draw back and separate himself from the Gentiles because he was afraid of those who belonged to the circumcision group. The other Jews joined him in his hypocrisy, so that by their hypocrisy even Barnabas was led astray.

When I saw that they were not acting in line with the truth of the gospel, I said to Cephas in front of them all, "You are a Jew, yet you live like a Gentile and not like a Jew. How is it, then, that you force Gentiles to follow Jewish customs?" (Gal. 2:11-14)

- **They correct sin, such as the Corinthian man who was sleeping with his stepmother:**

It is actually reported that there is sexual immorality among you, and of a kind that even pagans do not tolerate: A man is sleeping with his father's wife. And you are proud! Shouldn't you rather have gone into mourning and have put out of your fellowship the man who has been doing this? For my part, even though I am not physically present, I am with you in spirit. As one who is present with you in this way, I have already passed judgment in the name of our Lord Jesus on the one who has been doing this. (1 Cor. 5:1-3)

Most of the modern church has operated under the pastoral church model, which does not even allow the possibility of apostles existing today. With the pastoral model as the foundation, the main concern becomes caring for the sheep. That is why we do not see the strong types of correction we read about in the three examples above in the modern church. If a church is built on the apostolic model, then we will see issues being confronted and dealt with much more assertively because the comfort of the sheep is not the main concern.

We have followed the "pastor-like" model for centuries, but we need to restore the "apostle-like" model. All fivefold are to be apostle-like. Apostles are not supposed to be like pastors, but pastors are supposed to be like apostles. The apostles were the models, beginning with Jesus Himself, and then the twelve.

2. They Are Wise Master Builders

Some Christians get upset at the idea that we are called to build the church or advance the kingdom. They like to lean on the following verse as their proof text:

*And I tell you that you are Peter, and on this rock **I will build my church**, and the gates of Hades will not overcome it.* (Matt. 16:18)

"See," they say, "Jesus said He would build the church, so who are we to think that we are to build it?"

Yet Paul writes:

According to the grace of God which was given to me, like a wise master builder I laid a foundation, and another is building on it. But each man must be careful how he builds on it. (1 Cor. 3:10 NASB)

The right question to ask is: "*How* will Christ build His church?"

If a billionaire says he is going to build a hotel in Manhattan, you wouldn't expect to see him the next week in his new suit, on his hands and knees, trowel in hand, laying bricks.

Rather, you would expect him to call the best general contractor in the city to assemble a team, who would then build his hotel. The general contractor would be the "wise master builder" Paul claims he was. Apostles are the general contractors of the kingdom—the architects behind the entire building program.

I would extend this picture further to the other four graces. Each one would be like a different trade, for example:

- Prophets are the plumbers
- Evangelists are the electrical engineers
- Pastors are framers constructing the walls

---

[3] Any of the trades could be applied to any of the fivefold, for example, I am not trying to draw a deep connection between plumbers and Prophets.

Without the apostle acting as the architect, the other four graces will easily make mistakes and bring imbalance to the project. This is one of the reasons Paul said that apostles are first, prophets are second, and teachers are third (1 Cor. 12:28). There must be order to the fivefold for the church to be built right and for the kingdom to advance. Architects and general contractors are the ones who hold the blueprints for the project and give overall direction to the work.

Without architects, the church is like thousands of piles of bricks that gather each Sunday morning around the globe. But once an architect appears, those bricks begin to be put into place. We go from simply being a "gathering" of stones to being an "assembly."[4] This is the same metaphor used in the New Testament:

> *"you also, like living stones, are being built into a spiritual house to be a holy priesthood, offering spiritual sacrifices acceptable to God through Jesus Christ."* (1 Peter 2:5)

> *"Consequently, you are no longer foreigners and strangers, but fellow citizens with God's people and also members of his household, built on the foundation of the apostles and prophets, with Christ Jesus himself as the chief cornerstone. In him the whole building is joined together and rises to become a holy temple in the Lord. And in him you too are being built together to become a dwelling in which God lives by his Spirit."* (Eph. 2:19-22)

Christ is the chief cornerstone and the apostles and prophets are the foundation, yet we learned that the apostles also lay foundations

---

[4] This insight about moving from gathering to assembly is originally from Dr. Harold Eberle.

(see 1 Cor. 3:10). They are foundational and they lay foundations for others to build on.

3. *They Reproduce After Their Kind*

This is a principle in all of nature, but also in the kingdom. Each of the fivefold adjusts others into operating in their particular grace. Prophets get you prophesying, evangelists get you reaching the lost, pastors get you caring for other sheep, and teachers get you into the depths of the Word.

Then there is the apostle, who raises up apostles and the other fivefold. Apostles are focused on leadership and not directly focused on the saints. Wherever Paul and Barnabas went in the New Testament, they were raising up the saints who were called into the grace of leadership. Even in the apostolic letters from Paul to the apostles Titus and Timothy, we find that he instructs them to be putting others into positions of leadership (Titus 1:5; 2 Tim. 2:2). All fivefold reproduce after their own kind, but the apostle specifically reproduces other apostles as well as the other four graces. One implication of this is that pastors don't make apostles. This creates a problem when we build the church on the pastoral foundation: apostles end up aborted in embryo form, which not only eliminates apostles, but also hinders the other fivefold graces from being raised up in the church.

At this point, you might be asking: How do we know that apostles raise up the other four of the fivefold? Well, we have to look at the fivefold origin story. When the New Testament opens, apostles and evangelists don't exist yet, there were no prophets operating, and the spiritual shepherds and teachers of Israel had degenerated into the corrupt priesthood system.

Then the Messiah appeared. As I stated at the beginning of the chapter, Jesus Himself was a new breed of minister known as an apostle: *"Fix your thoughts on Jesus, whom we acknowledge as our apostle and high priest"* (Heb. 3:1b). As an apostle, Jesus replicated

Himself in twelve apostles (Luke 6:12-13), and the early church was built on the model of the twelve (Acts 2:42). New covenant prophets, evangelists, pastors, and teachers only came along later as they sprang up from the apostles' foundation.

The first evangelist in the New Testament, Philip, appears in Acts 8, when he goes to Samaria and a revival breaks out. Philip was one of the seven chosen to serve tables as a deacon. The apostles pray and lay hands on him in Acts 6:6, and the next time we hear about him, he is causing a move of God in Samaria. Then he is supernaturally picked up and moved by the Holy Spirit to lead the Ethiopian eunuch to Jesus.

The persecution that scattered Christians after the stoning of Stephen caused conversions to happen in Antioch. Then Barnabas (a prophet at the time) was sent up to Antioch from Jerusalem. He went and retrieved Saul of Tarsus, and they worked together teaching in Antioch for a year. Then more prophets, including Agabus, came down from Jerusalem for a visit (all of this is found in Acts 11:19-30).

By the time we get to Acts 13, Antioch has a well-established leadership of prophets, and the first teachers mentioned after the Day of Pentecost have now appeared!

What is important to note here is that the Jerusalem apostles raised up Barnabas the prophet, and he then raised up other prophets in Antioch. Eventually, those Antioch prophets declare him and Saul to be apostles and send them out (Acts 13:1-3).

When Paul was in Miletus in Acts 20:17, he sent for the Ephesian elders and spoke to them of his departure to Jerusalem and how they would never see him again. At that point, he commanded them to take care of God's flock and to be shepherds ("shepherd" shares the same root word as "pastor"). Paul raised them up during his three years of teaching in Ephesus, and then he released them with this first mention of pastoring. Again, we also find that Paul wrote to Timothy and Titus, giving them detailed instructions as young apostles, including who to raise up and who to lay hands on for commissioning into church leadership (1 Tim. 3, 5:17-22; Titus 1:5-9).

So we see that the apostles were the seedbed of the other four of the fivefold.

4. The Fivefold Are Model Christians

I began this chapter talking about how we are called to be like Jesus. That is a point that rarely engenders any debate. Yet there is another valid point, which is often overlooked. The apostles and fivefold leadership are designed to be models of Christlikeness, which we are to imitate.

I have a whole host of Scriptures below that I would encourage you to read through carefully. As you do, let this truth sink into your heart: Not all Christians are imitation-worthy, but fivefold leaders are specifically meant to be the model Christians for the rest of us.

I am writing this not to shame you but to warn you as my dear children. Even if you had ten thousand guardians in Christ, you do not have many fathers, for in Christ Jesus I became your father through the gospel. **Therefore I urge you to imitate me.** *For this reason I have sent to you Timothy, my son whom I love, who is faithful in the Lord. He will remind you of* **my way of life** *in Christ Jesus, which agrees with what I teach everywhere in every church.* (1 Cor. 4:14-17)

Imitate me, just as I also imitate Christ. (1 Cor. 11:1)

Join together in following my example, *brothers and sisters, and just as* **you have us as a model, keep your eyes on those who live as we do.** (Phil. 3:17)

You became imitators of us *and of the Lord, for you welcomed the message in the midst of severe suffering with the joy given by the Holy Spirit.* ***And so you became a model to all the believers*** *in Macedonia and Achaia.* (1 Thess. 1:6-7)

For you, brothers and sisters, became ***imitators*** *of God's churches in Judea, which are in Christ Jesus: You suffered from your own people the same things those churches suffered from the Jews.* (1 Thess. 2:14)

In the name of the Lord Jesus Christ, we command you, brothers and sisters, to ***keep away from every believer who*** *is idle and disruptive and* ***does not live according to the teaching you received from us.*** *For you yourselves know how you ought to* ***follow our example. . . .*** *We did this, not because we do not have the right to such help, but in order to offer ourselves as* ***a model for you to imitate.*** (2 Thess. 3: 6-7, 9)

Don't let anyone look down on you because you are young, but ***set an example*** *for the believers in speech, in conduct, in love, in faith and in purity.* (1 Tim. 4:12)

In everything set them an example *by doing what is good.* (Titus 2:7a)

We do not want you to become lazy, but to ***imitate those*** *who through faith and patience inherit what has been promised.* (Heb. 6:12)

> **Remember your leaders**, *who spoke the word of God to you. Consider the outcome of their way of life and* **imitate their faith.** (Heb. 13:7)

> *...not lording it over those entrusted to you, but* **being examples to the flock.** (1 Peter 5:3)

> *Dear friend, do not* **imitate** *what is evil but* **what is good.** *Anyone who does what is good is from God. Anyone who does what is evil has not seen God.* (3 John 1:11)

While reading these verses in the New Testament, I came to a realization. The apostle Paul didn't expect everyone to have a personal copy of his letters, which they would then memorize and quote to each other (which is what we do with the New Testament). Rather, Paul seemed to expect that people would read his *life* as the model. He himself was a letter, a model, and an example—someone worthy of imitating.

All Christian leaders should be able to confidently (and humbly) say, "Read my life, follow my example, and imitate me. If you want to be like Jesus, be like me!" If you cannot say this about yourself to your followers, then you probably shouldn't be leading.

Is your foundation strong? Is the fruit of your leadership feeding those who follow you? In your life and leadership, choose to imitate Christ—and in doing so, to live as an example for others to imitate.

CHAPTER TWO

FIVEFOLD MYTHS

Before I go further, I need to address some myths that are hindering the full expression of the fivefold ministry.

Most people retain unexamined assumptions about the fivefold—from what an evangelist does to the way a local pastor leads a church. These assumptions grow into myths, and myths by definition are widely held but false beliefs. For the church to move forward in the fivefold ministry, it is vital that we replace these myths with truth.

Here are some myths that need busting.

MYTH #1: *There were only twelve apostles, plus Paul.*

To dispel this myth, we need to look at the New Testament and see if there were any apostles other than the original twelve. A complete listing of New Testament apostles follows:

- Matthias, the replacement for Judas (Acts 1:23-26)
- James, the half brother of Jesus and leader of the Jerusalem church (Gal. 1:19)

- Barnabas (Acts 14:14)
- Paul (Acts 14:14 and many other references)
- Apollos (1 Cor. 4:6-9)
- Timothy and Silvanus (I Thess. 1:1 and 2:6)
- Andronicus and Junia: outstanding among the apostles (Rom. 16:7)
- Epaphroditus: While the King James Version translates the word as "messenger," the Greek word (*apostolon*) is actually "apostle" (Phil. 2:25)
- Two unnamed apostles: A brother of fame among the churches, and a brother tested, *"As for our brethren, they are messengers of the churches, a glory to Christ"* (2 Cor. 8:23). Again, the Greek word is *apostoloi*, but is translated here as "messengers."
- Jesus Himself (Heb. 3:1)

Twelve original apostles plus thirteen more named in the New Testament equals *twenty-five* apostles.

An investigation of the New Testament more than doubles the number of those who are explicitly referred to as apostles. Yet at no point are these extra twelve referred to or treated as "lesser" than the original twelve. In fact, it was one of the original twelve who got Jesus crucified and one of the extra twelve (Paul) who wrote one third of the New Testament. Only the modern mind sees current apostles as "lesser" than original apostles. Their function is the same, their grace is the same, and their calling is the same (except that modern apostles are not writing Scripture, but not all of the original apostles even wrote Scripture, so it never was a requirement).

Some theologians have categorized apostles, and it may be helpful to some to see these categories:

- Jesus the Chief Apostle (Heb. 3:1)
- The Apostles of the Lamb (Rev. 21:14)
- The Post-Ascension Apostles (Eph. 4:8-13)

MYTH #2: *Apostles and prophets no longer exist.*

There is no verse that explicitly states the cessation of apostles and prophets; in fact, there are verses that state quite the opposite.

Ephesians 4:13 opens by stating that the five graces are here "until." The word "until" is a time indicator, and it is followed by three conditions: the unity of the faith, knowledge and maturity, and attainment of the fullness of Christ. As these conditions have yet to be fulfilled in the body of Christ, we should expect that apostles and prophets, along with the other graces, need to be functioning in the church.

The fact that Ephesians 4:11-13 speaks of apostles and prophets given after the ascension of Christ shows that the original twelve apostles are not in view in Ephesians 4. Likewise, in His message to the church at Ephesus in Revelation 2:2, Jesus states: "I know your deeds, your hard work and your perseverance. I know that you cannot tolerate wicked people, that you have tested those who claim to be apostles but are not, and have found them false."

Jesus commended the Ephesian church for testing those who claimed to be apostles and finding them to be false. If there were to be no more apostles after the first batch, then the test would have been as easy as asking, "Are you one of the original twelve or Paul? No? Then you are not an apostle!" Clearly it was expected that there would be further apostles and that they should be examined.

1 Corinthians 12:28 uses the word "set" to describe the ordained role of apostles: *"God has set in the church firstly apostles, second prophets…"* This is the Greek word *tithemi*, which means "to set, fix, establish." The position of apostles in the church was not a temporary

position for the first century. It is a permanent fixture of biblical Christianity.

There is literally nothing to indicate that apostles and prophets have passed away, while evangelists, pastors, and teachers continue.

MYTH #3: *Apostles must see Jesus personally.*

This is based on a misunderstanding of 1 Corinthians 9:1:

> *Am I not free? Am I not an apostle? Have I not seen Jesus our Lord? Are you not the result of my work in the Lord?*

Some have taken this verse to mean that to be a true apostle, one must see Jesus. Yet Paul wasn't trying to qualify himself as an apostle. He was stating his qualifications as the apostle to Corinth. He wasn't writing a list of what qualifies someone as an apostle; he was qualifying himself as "their apostle." It's actually a list of four rhetorical questions. Paul says he is free, he is an apostle, he has seen the Lord, and the Corinthian believers are the fruit of his ministry. If one can argue that one must see the Lord to be an apostle, then one could argue that someone is an apostle simply because they are "free."

MYTH #4: *Paul said he was the last apostle.*

This myth comes from an oversimplified reading of 1 Corinthians 15:5-9:[5]

---

[5] "Paul's remark in 1 Corinthians 15:9 suggests that he saw himself as being the last and final apostle—at least the last of a certain type of apostle." R. Douglas Geivett, Holly Pivec, *God's Super-Apostles: Encountering the Worldwide Prophets and Apostles Movement* (Wooster, OH: Weaver Book Company, 2014), Kindle Location 503.

[He] appeared to Cephas [Peter], *then to the twelve. Then he appeared to more than five hundred brothers at one time, most of whom are still alive, though some have fallen asleep. Then he appeared to James, then to all the apostles.* **Last of all, as to one untimely born, he appeared also to me.** *For I am the least of the apostles, unworthy to be called an apostle, because I persecuted the church of God.* (1 Cor. 15: 5–9)

Paul is not stating that He was the last apostle based on seeing Jesus. He is referring to the circumstances around his salvation experience and how unique his salvation was. The Greek word Paul uses, *ektroma*, is translated here as, "untimely born," but it could also be translated as an "abortive birth" or "miscarriage." *Ektroma* is used only once in the New Testament. Here is its definition in Thayer's Lexicon:

ἔκτρωμα, ἔκτρωτος, τό (ἐκτιτρώσκω to cause or to suffer abortion; like ἔκβρωμα from ἐκβιβρώσκω), **an abortion, abortive birth; an untimely birth:** *1 Corinthians 15:8, where Paul likens himself to an* ἔκτρωμα, *and in 1 Corinthians 15:9 explains in what sense: that he is as inferior to the rest of the apostles as an immature birth comes short of a mature one, and is no more worthy of the name of an apostle than an abortion is of the name of a child.* (Numbers 12:12; Ecclesiastes 6:3; Job 3:16)

So Paul is being extremely denigrating of himself, but he is not trying to make an argument for how he was the last apostle, or the last one to see Jesus.

MYTH #5: *A person can carry all fivefold gifts and switch among them as needed.*

Let's debunk this myth Scripture by Scripture.

Ephesians 4:11: *"And He Himself gave some to be apostles, some prophets, some evangelists, and some pastors and teachers . . ."* (NKJV). This verse states in no uncertain terms that "some" are given as apostles, "some" as prophets, "some" as evangelists, etc. This shows that other than Jesus, none of us operates in all five gifts.

1 Corinthians 12:28: *"And God has placed in the church first of all apostles, second prophets, third teachers . . ."* Since Paul lists them in order, this indicates that not all of us are apostles, and not all are prophets.

James 3:1: *"Not many of you should become teachers, my fellow believers, because you know that we who teach will be judged more strictly."* Not everyone is a fivefold teacher, and you can't simply become one as needed. It is an actual calling and grace, and it should be taken on carefully.

Acts 13:1-3: *"Now in the church at Antioch there were prophets and teachers: Barnabas . . . and Saul. While they were worshiping the Lord and fasting, the Holy Spirit said, 'Set apart for me Barnabas and Saul for the work to which I have called them.' So after they had fasted and prayed, they placed their hands on them and sent them off."* Paul and Barnabas transitioned into becoming apostles. It was significant and serious. It involved group fasting, prayer, and the commissioning with the laying on of hands. They remained apostles for the rest of their lives. An individual can shift from one fivefold calling to another, but this is a serious shift and not something that happens regularly or casually.

1 Corinthians 12:17-20: *"If the whole body were an eye, where would the sense of hearing be? If the whole body were an ear, where would the sense of smell be?"* This is straightforward; we are not all an eye, nor all an ear. Just like different parts of the body function in specific ways, different parts of the fivefold function in specific ways.

1 Corinthians 12:29: *"Are all apostles? Are all prophets? Are all teachers? Do all work miracles?"* Paul's rhetorical questions remind us, again, that these are separate giftings.

As we can see from these verses, the fivefold graces do not switch from day to day, and nobody is walking in all five on an "as needed" basis. Also, not everyone is some type of the fivefold. Some are called to "equip the saints," and some are called to be "the saints." What is needed is the individual fivefold gifts working together in the family of the kingdom.

MYTH #6: Apostles are aged ministers with loads of experience.

In the Old Testament, the priests served from ages thirty to fifty. In the contemporary church, the idea of a thirty-year-old apostle scares a lot of people. Yet Jesus Himself was a thirty-year-old apostle. As the rabbi of His twelve apostles, He would have been their elder spiritually and physically. According to many scholars, Jesus' twelve apostles were likely under the age of twenty, except for Peter.[6]

MYTH #7: It is rare to find all fivefold ministers in one local congregation.

There are more fivefold-graced leaders than many people realize. *"Two or three prophets should speak, and the others should weigh carefully what is said"* (1 Cor. 14:29). In Corinth alone, there were so many fivefold prophets that there was only time for two or three of them to speak at a church meeting, while the other prophets listened to and judged their words. That is a lot of prophets in one church!

[6] In Exodus 30:14-15, Jewish law states that every male over the age of twenty is to pay a half-shekel as a census offering when he visits the temple of God. In Matthew 17:24-27, Jesus instructs Peter to "fish up" this tax, and to find a four-drachma coin in the mouth of the fish he catches—enough to pay the tax for two men, himself and Jesus. Jesus requests this only for Peter and for Jesus. It is most likely that the others were underage and did not need to pay.

Based on my observations, I would conjecture that in an average group of 20-25 church people, there is typically one fivefold minister. This means that in the average church of 150 members, it would be normal to find all fivefold graces present. This doesn't mean that all people graced with the fivefold should be on paid staff at a church. Many fivefold leaders will maintain a normal job, and yet they will operate in their grace in the local church context.

It seems best to identify the prophet, evangelist, pastor, and teacher first, and to begin by having them study and develop their gifting. Many times, by focusing on the other four graces first, the apostle is then discovered. The apostle will be the one who is pushing the other four toward their callings and helping drive the leaders forward. This individual may not actually attend the local church. Many churches will function with the other four graces, receiving periodical input from an itinerant apostle.

MYTH #8: *Every local church needs an apostle.*

Not everyone needs an apostle installed as a leader in their local church. However, it is important that every local church has a relationship with an apostle.

Apostles are the highest authority in the church (1 Cor. 12:28), which means they have the highest calling to foot-washing in the body of Christ (John 13). This typically means that apostles will stand behind and raise up prophets, evangelists, pastors, and teachers.

This is important enough to repeat: Apostles are both foot-washers *and* the highest authority in the church. They clarify, confirm, and announce the callings and grace on the lives of newer apostles as well as prophets, evangelists, pastors, and teachers. They establish the leadership of the body of Christ with proper structure and order. For example, Timothy and Titus were both younger apostles, and Paul was a senior apostle who guided and affirmed them.

In many ways, an apostle is like a good father. A good father guides, instructs, affirms, provides, and backs you up. He *does not* control you, manipulate you, lord his authority over you, or only claim that you are his kid when it makes him look good, while refusing to answer your calls when you need him. Many modern "apostles" are more like the bad father. This has cast a terrible light upon apostleship.

However, apostles are not personal prayer partners and private Bible study mentors. Many people with an orphan mentality have hoped that an apostle would come along and be their private mentor and constant coach. Apostles guide the leaders of the church, not typically those who aren't walking in a fivefold calling.

Once we break out of the reductionist perspective, which sees the fivefold grace as extremely rare, we will find God has given us an abundant supply of leaders who need to be developed and recognized in our midst. This doesn't mean that the apostle is a local member, but that the church is in relationship with an apostle for his or her grace to impact the church.

MYTH #9: We do not need to acknowledge fivefold titles.

The early church seemed at ease with correctly identifying people by their grace and calling. For example, Paul starts nine of his thirteen letters by saying, "Paul, an apostle." Peter does the same with both of his letters.

Confusion regarding the use of biblical titles and terminology has caused two main problems. While many leaders have misused the title of apostle for various reasons (ego, control, etc.), the rest of the leadership in the body of Christ has been called by the broad term "pastor." Pastor is a title that is used once in the English translation of the Bible (Eph. 4:11), a title that has no explanation and no named New Testament example. This has led to many apostles, prophets, evangelists, and teachers being underdeveloped, unrecognized, overlooked, unacknowledged, and dishonored.

This is a significant problem because what we honor in someone's life is what we draw from them. As Jesus said: "Whoever welcomes a prophet as a prophet will receive a prophet's reward . . ." (Matt. 10:41). One implication of this statement is, *"Whoever receives a prophet as a pastor will simply receive confusion."* We must begin to actually identify what people are walking in so that we can draw it out of them through honor. If we continue to only acknowledge and honor "pastors," the body of Christ will be in confusion and will dishonor four of the five graces (Eph. 4:11).

Titles can also be helpful for introducing a leader to a new group of people. In that moment, the words we choose will create a platform of respect in the atmosphere for others to receive and pull on the grace on the person's life. If we say, "Allow me to introduce Prophet Joe," then people will begin to pull on the grace of a prophet. Or if we say, "This is Teacher Joe," then people will pull on that grace. Identifying graces will give people the opportunity to pull on these graces.

MYTH #10: People who claim to be apostles are arrogant.

You might have heard this cliché: "If you call yourself an apostle, then you probably aren't one." This rubbish would actually disqualify the leaders who wrote the New Testament. Let us abandon such silly generalizations and rather be more accurate by saying, "If you are arrogant, you may still be an apostle, but you need to humble yourself."

It is important to understand that there have always been "false apostles" (Rev. 2:2) and people who have simply grabbed a title to give themselves a sense of superiority (2 Cor. 11:5).

I believe that God is raising up and revealing genuine apostles. I also believe many people have assumed that the title of apostle would give them a greater sense of power. Basically, I don't acknowledge "apostles" who are not washing the feet of the leaders in the body of Christ.

Here are two typical scenarios in the church today: After decades of pastoral ministry, many senior pastors retire from their church and try to go on the road as itinerant apostles, or they stay with their former church and keep control of the new pastor by taking on the title of "apostle overseer" or "apostolic leader." Such scenarios have caused a lot of confusion regarding the function of actual apostles. The role of an apostle is not something that you "graduate into" after so many years as a pastor.

Those who are true apostles see the big picture from the highest vantage point. This is evident in the early church, as we see in the book of Acts. When the Gentiles started to get saved and filled with the Holy Spirit, the apostle James led a council in Jerusalem. It was here that the apostles Paul and Peter came and weighed in regarding Gentile salvation. Thanks to James, Paul, and Peter, the early church was able to grasp the larger picture of what God was doing in the earth. That ability is uniquely apostolic.

Prophets can declare the future, give courage, and comfort, yet they often only see through a specific lens the Lord has given them. They need apostles to help them see the larger picture and how their prophetic insight works in the larger scheme of what the Lord is doing.

Evangelists are focused on saving souls, yet they need the apostolic to help balance active evangelism with effective church structure so that new converts have a place to grow.

Pastors shepherd the hearts of people, yet they need the apostolic to provoke them to build their people into advancers of the kingdom (1 Tim. 1:4). Apostles stretch and challenge the sheep to stay healthy and not settle into a comfort zone.

Teachers build structures of sound thinking, yet they need apostles to keep them reaching beyond the natural for the supernatural. Apostles stretch teachers and keep them from settling for a good theory. Apostles push teachers to become a living manifestation of their good teaching (1 Tim 4:13-14).

These are some of the practical ways that, through relationship, an apostle can "wash the feet" of the other fivefold gifts. It is also why the apostle is first (1 Cor. 12:28), because they are pulling up other leaders to see from their vantage point.

MYTH #11: *Some apostles operate outside of the church.*

I have been doing a heavy study of the fivefold ministry both in Scripture and in the writings of modern teachers, and I keep coming across modern writers mentioning "apostles in the marketplace." The definitions seem a bit unclear so far, but essentially these "apostles" are influential Christians who think like kings and are wise with finances.

Because there is so much confusion regarding what an actual apostle is, these wonderful individuals are being called "marketplace apostles." Typically, these "marketplace apostles" are not actually doing the work of a biblical "apostle" per se, but we haven't known how to classify them, so we made up a term that actually causes more confusion and waters down the definition of a true apostle.

Some signs of true apostles:

- Signs, wonders, and miracles
- Supernatural revelation and insight
- Correcting false doctrine
- Raising and releasing other fivefold ministers
- Traveling to establish churches and ministries
- Patiently enduring hatred and persecution
- Being set apart and sent to grow the universal church (not focused entirely on the local church)

These are the characteristics I have seen among the twenty-five apostles named in Scripture. I have *not* seen modern "marketplace apostles" who fit in this description.

I see the role of the fivefold ministry as equipping, and the apostle's role is specifically to equip and raise up the other four of the fivefold. We need apostles actually doing what apostles should do.

I would suggest that those we are currently calling "marketplace apostles" are not apostles at all, but are actually gifted with the Romans 12:8 gifts of leadership and/or generosity.

In Conclusion

A myth is a myth. And these specific myths have hindered the church's power. Let's be willing to press in for the truth, free the fivefold from wrong assumptions, and honor their gifts for the advancement of the kingdom.

CHAPTER THREE

METRONS AND GRACES

God assigns a sphere of influence to each fivefold minister. Nobody is pastor of the whole world or apostle of the planet. We each have been given a sphere of influence and the grace needed for that specific sphere. Paul wrote of this in 2 Corinthians:

> We, however, will not boast beyond proper limits, but will confine our boasting to the **sphere** of service God himself has assigned to us, a **sphere** that also includes you. We are not going too far in our boasting, as would be the case if we had not come to you, for we did get as far as you with the gospel of Christ. Neither do we go beyond our limits by boasting of work done by others. Our hope is that, as your faith that is continues to grow, our **sphere** of activity among you will greatly expand, so that we can preach the gospel in the regions beyond you. For we do not want to boast about work already done in someone else's territory. (2 Cor. 10:13-17)

Paul specifically says that he will not boast beyond proper limits, which is to say that his sphere of influence had limits, but within those limits was the Corinthian church—they were part of his assigned sphere of influence. Paul also mentions that as the faith of the Corinthians grew, his sphere of activity would also greatly expand. He says it another way in his first letter to the Corinthians:

> *Even though I may not be an apostle to others, surely I am to you! For you are the seal of my apostleship in the Lord.* (1 Cor. 9:2)

Paul was not an apostle to everyone; he was only an apostle to those in his God-assigned sphere of influence.

It is imperative for fivefold ministers to understand the boundary lines of their sphere of influence. Most church leadership conflicts are rooted in not understanding these boundary lines.

METRON

The Greek root word translated "sphere" is the word *metron*, which is also sometimes translated in the New Testament as "measure." If you are an apostle, you must understand where your metron begins and ends. Not every church you walk into has to accept you as an apostle. Paul knew he was an apostle to the Corinthians because they were in his metron. If you are the pastor of a congregation, that doesn't mean that you are the pastor of every congregation that you walk into. This principle was taught by Jesus in the Gospels:

> *Whoever welcomes a prophet as a prophet will receive a prophet's reward, and whoever welcomes a righteous person as a righteous person will receive a righteous person's reward.* (Matt. 10:41)

Those in a metron must receive you and honor you for the grace on your life to flow to them. If you are the pastor of your congregation, then your members have received you as such, and the pastoral grace flows from your life and impacts them. But if an unknown prophet shows up one Sunday morning and begins to prophesy over people in the foyer, this would be a boundary violation. People do not know this individual and have not honored him as a prophet, and he is basically casting his metron over people like an unwelcomed net. Yet that prophet could be known and honored and received in other situations where he legitimately has the right to operate because he is in his metron. Alternatively, a pastor could invite a prophet from out of town and ask him to minister on a Sunday morning, in which case the pastor is giving the prophet the right to minister in his metron of influence. And as the pastor introduces the guest prophet, he can lay a platform of honor so that his people can receive the grace on the life of the guest prophet.

We see in Paul's writings that he was keenly aware of his metron and the metron of others. Paul's specific metron was the Gentiles; Peter's was the Jews:

Through him we received grace and apostleship to call all the Gentiles to the obedience that comes from faith for his name's sake. (Rom. 1:5)

For God, who was at work in Peter as an apostle to the circumcised, was also at work in me as an apostle to the Gentiles. (Gal. 2:8)

Yet I have written you quite boldly on some points to remind you of them again, because of the grace God gave me to be a minister of Christ Jesus to the Gentiles. He gave me the priestly duty of proclaiming the gospel of God, so that the Gentiles might become an offering acceptable to God, sanctified by the Holy Spirit. (Rom. 15:15-16)

GRACE

There is neither Jew nor Gentile, neither slave nor free, nor is there male and female, for you are all one in Christ Jesus. (Gal. 3:28)

One of the beautiful things that the new covenant accomplished was the restoring of equality among all people. Yet that restoration does not change the fact that men and women still exist with distinct differences, and that Paul was called to the Gentiles while Peter was called to the Jews. Equality is restored, but distinctions remain.

Another important truth is that although in Christ, we are all equal, in grace we are *not all equal.* I am not speaking of saving grace, which is poured out equally to all (Titus 2:11); I am speaking of the empowering grace for fivefold leadership. This is a unique measure of grace that is given specifically for you to minister to your metron. (You do not have grace to operate outside of your metron.)

For example, not every disciple was given the metron and grace of being an apostle. Jesus spent an entire night in prayer before He put apostolic grace on twelve individuals:

One of those days Jesus went out to a mountainside to pray, and spent the night praying to God. When morning came, he called his disciples to him and chose twelve of them, whom he also designated apostles. (Luke 6:12-13)

And why was this taken so seriously? Because grace has a weight to it. The grace of being an apostle in the first century could literally kill you. Jesus knew that these particular followers would end up martyred because He put apostolic grace on their lives. The exceptions were Judas, who still died by suicide, and John, who, tradition tells us, was unable to be martyred.

The impartation of fivefold grace for leadership is deadly important. It should be taken seriously—perhaps with all-night prayer sessions or even fasting, as happened in Antioch when Paul and Barnabas were supernaturally given grace, which made them into apostles:

> *While they were worshiping the Lord and fasting, the Holy Spirit said, "Set apart for me Barnabas and Saul for the work to which I have called them." So after they had fasted and prayed, they placed their hands on them and sent them off.* (Acts 13:2-3)

After Paul and Barnabas were launched as apostles, they were also very serious about placing grace upon others. We see this when they installed leaders in Lystra, Iconuim, and Antioch—also with prayer and fasting:

> *Paul and Barnabas appointed elders for them in each church and, with prayer and fasting, committed them to the Lord, in whom they had put their trust.* (Acts 14:23)

Later, the apostle Paul gave directions to the apostle Titus saying that he left him in Crete specifically to ordain leaders:

> *The reason I left you in Crete was that you might put in order what was left unfinished and ordain elders in every town, as I directed you.* (Titus 1:5)

This is the serious business of fivefold ministers: to carefully distribute the impartation of grace and raise up new leaders within their own metrons.

It is important to understand our metrons—the boundaries where our influence begins and ends—yet it is just as important to understand that grace is what empowers us to take care of our metron. Notice that when Paul spoke with authority to those in his metron, he specifically made mention of the grace on his life, which was the grace of an apostle:

> *I became a servant of this gospel by **the gift of God's grace given me** through the working of his power. Although I am less than the least of all the Lord's people, **this grace was given me: to preach to the Gentiles** the boundless riches of Christ . . .* (Eph. 3:7-8)

> *For **by the grace given me** I say to every one of you: Do not think of yourself more highly than you ought, but rather think of yourself with sober judgment, in accordance with the faith God has distributed to each of you.* (Rom. 12:3)

> ***By the grace God has given me**, I laid a foundation as a wise builder, and someone else is building on it. But each one should build with care.* (1 Cor. 3:10)

Paul actually attributes his hard work to the grace that was on his life:

> ***But by the grace of God** I am what I am, and his grace to me was not without effect. No, **I worked harder than all of them—yet not I, but the grace of God** that was with me.* (1 Cor. 15:10)

The author of Hebrews even says that Jesus died for us because of the grace that empowered Him!

*But we do see Jesus, who was made lower than the angels for a little while, now crowned with glory and honor because he suffered death, so that **by the grace of God** he might taste death for everyone.* (Heb. 2:9)

Before we leave the topic of metrons, we should ask a question: Do only fivefold leaders have metrons, or do metrons apply to all people?

The other place that Paul writes about "metrons" is in Ephesians 4, the section about the fivefold:

But to each one of us grace was given according to the measure **[metron]** *of Christ's gift.* (Eph. 4:7)

And He gave some as apostles, and some as prophets, and some as evangelists, and some as pastors and teachers, for the equipping of the saints for the work of service, to the building up of the body of Christ; until we all attain to the unity of the faith, and of the knowledge of the Son of God, to a mature man, to the measure **[metron]** *of the stature which belongs to the fullness of Christ.* (Eph. 4:11-13)

Then we will no longer be infants, tossed back and forth by the waves, and blown here and there by every wind of teaching and by the cunning and craftiness of people in their deceitful scheming. Instead, speaking the truth in love, we will grow to become in every respect the mature body of him who is the head, that is, Christ. From him the whole body, joined and held together by every supporting ligament, grows and builds itself up in love, as each part **[metron]** *does its work.* (Eph. 4:14-16)

According to verse 16, we have each been given a metron, and according to verse 7, we have the grace needed for our metron. Yet verses 11-13 show us that some have been given the grace of being an apostle, some have the grace of being a prophet, etc. And the end goal of those five graces is to bring the whole body of Christ into the full measure of *Jesus'* metron.

Jesus' metron is to be Lord of Lords and King of Kings, and all the kingdoms of this earth are to become the kingdom of our Lord (Rev. 11:15). The goal of the fivefold graces is to get every member of the body activated in caring for their metrons, so that the influence of the kingdom covers the whole world, until our metrons fully match the metron of Jesus.

The fivefold's metron is focused on maturing and adjusting the body of Christ. This will result in the whole body functioning properly and every metron doing its part until the kingdom of God on earth—through the influence of His people—matches His full metron in heaven. Although this message is true, many have distorted its implications and have become domineering. The bottom line is that we are to spread the kingdom with the same heart as our foot-washing, cosmic King.

GRACE OR ANOINTING?

Before I continue, I'd like to distinguish between grace and anointing.

There are nineteen references to "anointing" in the New Testament:

- Four refer to anointing the sick.
- Four refer to the spiritual anointing that was on Jesus.
- Two refer to anointing as an ordinary Jewish custom.

- Five refer to the anointing of Jesus, feet or His anointing for burial.

The remaining four mentions of anointing refer to the spiritual anointing on Christians. Here are those references in the New King James Version:

But you have an anointing from the Holy One, and you know all things. (1 John 2:20)

But the anointing which you have received from Him abides in you, and you do not need that anyone teach you; but as the same anointing teaches you concerning all things, and is true, and is not a lie, and just as it has taught you, you will abide in Him. (1 John 2:27)

Now He who establishes us with you in Christ and has anointed us is God, who also has sealed us and given us the Spirit in our hearts as a guarantee. (2 Cor. 1:21-22)

I counsel you to buy from Me gold refined in the fire, that you may be rich; and white garments, that you may be clothed, that the shame of your nakedness may not be revealed; and anoint your eyes with eye salve, that you may see. (Rev. 3:18)

There is major confusion in the modern church regarding "anointing." It is seen as something that comes when a minister stands behind a pulpit, or as the goosebumps that one feels when praying over others, or as the different types of giftings that flow from the Holy Spirit.

The Old Testament tells us a lot more about anointing than the New Testament does. Kings, prophets, and priests were all anointed in the Old Testament. The anointing did *not* come and go. It was applied and remained. Even in the case of evil King Saul, David recognized him as the Lord's "anointed" long after God had rejected him as the chosen king.

As a Christian, you have been smeared with the presence of the Holy Spirit. The word "anoint" means "to smear," so to be "anointed" is to have "been smeared" (past tense), and the "anointing" of the Holy Spirit is the "smearing" of the Holy Spirit. As a believer, you receive a smearing of the Holy Spirit's presence and power in your life. It isn't coming and going, or increasing and decreasing. You have an anointing that remains—"the anointing you received from him remains in you" (1 John 2:27 NIV).

Vine's Complete Expository Dictionary defines "to anoint" as: "A verb, to smear or consecrate. A common word in both ancient and modern Hebrew. . . It occurs approximately 70 times in the Hebrew Old Testament."[7] Mounce's Complete Expository Dictionary of Old Testament and New Testament words says, "The basic meaning of *masah* is to 'rub' with a liquid."[8]

The "anointing" is not a "thing"; rather, it is an action—a smearing. And grace is the actual content of the smearing. It is grace that is smeared (anointed) on to a person so that they are empowered for their metron to fulfill their particular unique calling.

Yes, there are different graces and different measures of grace that an individual can carry—and grace can increase on a person's life—but "anointing" is the wrong term to use.

It is important that we communicate clearly about spiritual realities, yet much of what is said about "anointing" is unbiblical and

[7] *Vine's Complete Expository Dictionary of Old and New Testament Words.* W. Vine, M. F. Unger, and W. White (Nashville, TN: Thomas Nelson, 1996), 5-6.

[8] *Mounce's Complete Expository Dictionary of Old Testament and New Testament Words,* William D. Mounce (Grand Rapids, MI: Zondervan, 2006), 23-24.

causes confusion. I believe it is wiser to remove "anointing" from much of our communication, and focus rather on what unique graces are on a person's life and their particular metron.

HUMILITY

Another important dynamic to understand is humility. Grace is given not only based on calling and metron, but also based on humility. Some are humble and receive more grace; some are arrogant and lose what they have:

> *Humble yourselves, therefore, under God's mighty hand, that he may lift you up in due time.* (1 Peter 5:6)

> *But He gives more grace. Therefore He says: "God resists the proud, but gives grace to the humble."* (James 4:6 NKJV)

As I've mentioned, grace has weight to it, and those who have developed "humility muscles" are those who can carry more without being crushed. Even James admonishes similarly: *"Not many of you should become teachers, my fellow believers, because you know that we who teach will be judged more strictly"* (James 3:1). The grace of being a teacher came with a higher weight of judgment on it.

We must approach our God-assigned metrons with humility. If you think *you can't do something*, but you are called to it, then you have the humility to receive an expanded metron from God and the grace to care for it.

For example, nobody knows how to be a parent or a spouse or a business owner until God expands their metron, at which point He gives them the grace needed to empower them for the task.

Humility leads to an expanded metron and an increase of grace to handle that expanded metron.

THE FLATTENED BODY

Honoring the grace we see on someone's life is how we receive the benefit of their grace into our own life. If we can recognize what grace and metron someone is walking in, then we can receive them properly and receive from them:

> *Whoever welcomes a prophet as a prophet will receive a prophet's reward, and whoever welcomes a righteous person as a righteous person will receive a righteous person's reward* (Matt. 10:41).

If we can't recognize unique graces on people's lives, then we will be lacking because of our inability to receive. Again, this is why it can be so helpful to actually use the titles of these five graces when introducing a fivefold minister. It helps others know how to receive the grace that is on their life.

Much of the modern church has been affected by a particular teaching that makes fivefold grace practically null and void. Many preachers have latched on to a "finished works" message (such as that which Joseph Prince or Andrew Wommack teaches; some also refer to this as the "grace movement"), which flattens the body. That message sounds good at first because it demolishes hierarchy and performance, but in the end, it removes the uniqueness of our identities and callings and the knowledge of how to steward our metrons and our graces—and how to receive grace from others. We must recognize that we are equal in Christ, but we do not have equal metrons, equal callings, or equal graces. This was Paul's point in 1 Corinthians 12:

*And God has placed in the church first of all apostles, second prophets, third teachers, then miracles, then gifts of healing, of helping, of guidance, and of different kinds of tongues. Are all apostles? Are all prophets? Are all teachers? Do all work miracles? Do all have gifts of healing? Do all speak in tongues? Do all interpret? Now eagerly **desire the greater gifts.***

And yet I will show you the most excellent way. (1 Cor. 12:28-31)

Paul ends his discussion on diversity in 1 Corinthians 12:12-31 by saying, "Desire the greater gifts." This shows us that some gifts are greater than others, which is an offensive statement to some, yet true nonetheless.

I also believe that we should want our metrons to grow larger and our grace empowerment to increase. Therefore our best plan is choosing to humble ourselves so that more grace comes into our life.

CHAPTER FOUR

SEVEN POINTS ABOUT METRONS

If you have a fivefold metron and grace on your life, then you will likely experience the following seven effects in your life.

1. You will care for the church.

> *I do not say this to condemn you; I have said before that **you have such a place in our hearts that we would live or die with you.*** (2 Cor. 7:3)

> *My dear children, **for whom I am again in the pains of childbirth** until Christ is formed in you, **how I wish I could be with you now** and change my tone, because I am perplexed about you!* (Gal. 4:19-20)

> **It is right for me to feel this way about all of you, since I have you in my heart** *and, whether I am in chains or defending and*

*confirming the gospel, all of you share in God's grace with me. God can testify **how I long for all of you with the affection of Christ Jesus*** (Phil. 1:7-8)

*Therefore, my brothers and sisters, you **whom I love and long for**, my joy and crown, stand firm in the Lord in this way, dear friends!* (Phil. 4:1)

*But, brothers and sisters, when we were **orphaned by being separated from you for a short time (in person, not in thought), out of our intense longing we made every effort to see you.** For we wanted to come to you—certainly I, Paul, did, again and again—but Satan blocked our way. For what is our hope, our joy, or the crown in which we will glory in the presence of our Lord Jesus when he comes? Is it not you? Indeed, you are our glory and joy.* (1 Thess. 2:17-20)

If your metron is not the church, then you will not relate to Paul's words. If you are graced with a fivefold grace, then you will have the same passion and love for God's people that Paul displays.

2. You will suffer immensely.

Are they servants of Christ? (I am out of my mind to talk like this.) I am more. I have worked much harder, been in prison more frequently, been flogged more severely, and been exposed to death again and again. Five times I received from the Jews the forty lashes minus one. Three times I was beaten with rods, once I was pelted with stones, three times I was shipwrecked, I spent a night and a day in the open sea, I have been constantly on the move. I have been in danger from rivers, in danger from bandits, in danger from my fellow Jews, in danger from Gentiles;

*in danger in the city, in danger in the country, in danger at sea; and in danger from false believers. I have labored and toiled and have often gone without sleep; I have known hunger and thirst and have often gone without food; I have been cold and naked. **Besides everything else, I face daily the pressure of my concern for all the churches.** Who is weak, and I do not feel weak? Who is led into sin, and I do not inwardly burn?* (2 Cor. 11:23-29)

Paul was treated horribly, yet in verse 28 he says that the worst thing he suffered was his own concern for the churches! When they were weak, he felt it; when they sinned, he felt it. His own love for God's people was the heaviest thing he endured.

For it seems to me that God has put us apostles on display at the end of the procession, like those condemned to die in the arena. We have been made a spectacle to the whole universe, to angels as well as to human beings. We are fools for Christ, but you are so wise in Christ! We are weak, but you are strong! You are honored, we are dishonored! To this very hour we go hungry and thirsty, we are in rags, we are brutally treated, we are homeless. We work hard with our own hands. When we are cursed, we bless; when we are persecuted, we endure it; when we are slandered, we answer kindly. We have become the scum of the earth, the garbage of the world—right up to this moment. (1 Cor. 4:9-13)

The fivefold graces, especially the apostles, are the lowest foot-washers on the planet. Being a fivefold leader means that you are signing up to suffer, not to be praised. Yes, some will honor you for your service to the kingdom, but the challenges faced by those with fivefold grace are immense:

*We do not want you to be uninformed, brothers and sisters, about the troubles we experienced in the province of Asia. **We were under great pressure, far beyond our ability to endure, so that we despaired of life itself. Indeed, we felt we had received the sentence of death.** But this happened that we might not rely on ourselves but on God, who raises the dead. He has delivered us from such a deadly peril, and he will deliver us again. On him we have set our hope that he will continue to deliver us, as you help us by your prayers. Then many will give thanks on our behalf for the gracious favor granted us in answer to the prayers of many.* (2 Cor. 1:8-11)

Even Paul despaired of life itself; it is only by true fivefold grace that a fivefold metron can be handled. For those who simply graduate from a seminary and then pastor a church without knowing about grace and metrons, the job can be incredibly dangerous. That is why hundreds of full-time ministers resign every month, and a majority of seminary graduates will quit after their first year and never re-enter full-time ministry. We need to rediscover the importance of receiving a supernatural impartation of grace and working within the boundaries of our God-assigned metrons.

3. You will build up those in your metron.

*So even if I boast somewhat freely about **the authority the Lord gave us for building you up** rather than tearing you down, I will not be ashamed of it.* (2 Cor. 10:8)

*This is why I write these things when I am absent, that when I come I may not have to be harsh in my use of authority—**the authority the Lord gave me for building you up**, not for tearing you down* (2 Cor. 13:10)

To the elders among you, I appeal as a fellow elder and a witness of Christ's sufferings who also will share in the glory to be revealed: **Be shepherds of God's flock that is under your care, watching over them**—*not because you must, but because you are willing, as God wants you to be; not pursuing dishonest gain, but* **eager to serve**; *not lording it over those entrusted to you, but* **being examples to the flock**. *And when the Chief Shepherd appears, you will receive the crown of glory that will never fade away.* (1 Peter 5:1-4)

The authority that God gives within fivefold grace is for building up those within your metron. It's for serving, laying your life down, sacrificing yourself, and being an example—not for tearing others down.

4. You will work hard.

He is the one we proclaim, admonishing and teaching everyone with all wisdom, so that we may present everyone fully mature in Christ. **To this end I strenuously contend with all the energy Christ so powerfully works in me.** (Col. 1:28-29)

Epaphras, who is one of you and a servant of Christ Jesus, sends greetings. **He is always wrestling in prayer for you**, *that you may stand firm in all the will of God, mature and fully assured.* (Col. 4:12)

Being a fivefold minister is not an easy gig. It is not glamorous or even enviable. It is brutal, hard work. It is having your arms thrust into the dirt and working the soil of the kingdom, getting up at four in the morning and "working the fields" until sundown. It is sweaty, bloody, dirty, tiring work to pour out your heart everywhere you go and to suffer on behalf of your calling. If anyone tells you otherwise, they are either lying or not doing true New Testament ministry. But with the grace of your metron, this hard work can be rewarding and not depleting.

5. You will raise others to care for your metron.

> *I hope in the Lord Jesus to send Timothy to you soon, that I also may be cheered when I receive news about you. I have no one else like him, who will show genuine concern for your welfare. For everyone looks out for their own interests, not those of Jesus Christ.* **But you know that Timothy has proved himself, because as a son with his father he has served with me in the work of the gospel.** *I hope, therefore, to send him as soon as I see how things go with me. And I am confident in the Lord that I myself will come soon.* (Phil. 2:19-24)

Paul raised up so many leaders that I will not even try to list them here. Suffice it to say that Timothy and Titus are probably the clearest examples of younger apostles whom Paul raised up. These beautiful leaders were able to carry on Paul's work in the hopes that his metron would be cared for after he was gone. This is what a good fivefold leader will do. Not only will they suffer for their metron and pour out their heart for their metron, but also they will want to set others in place so that kingdom momentum will not be lost.

6. The laying on of hands increases your metron.

> *While they were worshiping the Lord and fasting, the Holy Spirit said, "Set apart for me Barnabas and Saul for the work to*

which I have called them." So after they had fasted and prayed, they placed their hands on them and sent them off. (Acts 13:2-3)

Paul and Barnabas appointed elders for them in each church and, with prayer and fasting, committed them to the Lord, in whom they had put their trust. (Acts 14:23)

Do not neglect your gift, which was given you through prophecy when the body of elders laid their hands on you. (1 Tim. 4:14)

Do not be hasty in the laying on of hands, and do not share in the sins of others. Keep yourself pure. (1 Tim. 5:22)

The reason I left you in Crete was that you might put in order what was left unfinished and appoint elders in every town, as I directed you. (Titus 1:5)

I long to see you so that I may impart to you some spiritual gift to make you strong . . . (Rom. 1:11)

Although all believers are to lay their hands on the sick for supernatural healing to occur (Mark 16:18), a certain laying on of hands is meant to be done by leadership. It is an impartation of fivefold grace that comes upon a person who is also being acknowledged in their metron of fivefold calling. Those with a recognized fivefold metron and the accompanying grace are those who should be performing this type of impartation. This is not a ritual; it is an actual supernatural impartation event, and the receiver will be impacted and leave changed. Impartation is not simply a ceremony.

7. *You may have more than one metron or grace.*

Paul was not only an apostle, but also a teacher:

> *And of this gospel I was appointed a herald and **an apostle and a teacher**.* (2 Tim. 1:11)

Also, Timothy was known as both an apostle and an evangelist:

> *Paul, Silas and **Timothy**, To the church of the Thessalonians in God the Father and the Lord Jesus Christ: Grace and peace to you…. We were not looking for praise from people, not from you or anyone else, even though **as apostles** of Christ we could have asserted our authority* (1 Thess. 1:1, 2:6)

> *Preach the word; be prepared in season and out of season; correct, rebuke and encourage—with great patience and careful instruction. For the time will come when people will not put up with sound doctrine. Instead, to suit their own desires, they will gather around them a great number of teachers to say what their itching ears want to hear. They will turn their ears away from the truth and turn aside to myths. But you, keep your head in all situations, endure hardship, **do the work of an evangelist**, discharge all the duties of your ministry.* (2 Tim. 4:2-5)

Having more than one grace on your life is not uncommon, but it can also cause some confusion. Paul was probably known as a teacher for years before Antioch launched him as an apostle in Acts 13. But Paul probably felt the dual calling in his life before Acts 13. Although he was only a teacher at that point, he may have felt the tug of apostolic ministry; however, at the time, no one outside of the Jerusalem apostles had been given an apostolic metron or grace. I have met many people who feel a tug toward a particular fivefold grace, but they have not been given the God-assigned metron, and therefore the grace is not yet present.

For those who are feeling a tug toward a particular fivefold grace, it will take an understanding of metrons and grace—and the re-emergence of true apostles—to begin to put leaders into their God-assigned metrons and to impart grace to empower fivefold ministers. Thankfully, that is what the Holy Spirit is restoring in the earth in our day.

As a recap, here are the seven points to keep in mind as you grow in your understanding of metrons:

1. You will care for the church.
2. You will suffer immensely.
3. You will build up those in your metron.
4. You will work hard.
5. You will raise up others to care for your metron.
6. The laying on of hands increases your metron.
7. You may have more than one metron or grace.

CHAPTER FIVE

THE FIVEFOLD HEART:
Servant-Hearted, Transparent, Affectionate

And God has placed in the church first of all apostles, second prophets, third teachers, then miracles, then gifts of healing, of helping, of guidance, and of different kinds of tongues. (1 Cor. 12:28)

First apostles, second prophets, third teachers. Many have confused this passage with the idea of a fivefold hierarchy. Let's remember what Jesus said: *"So the last will be first, and the first will be last"* (Matt. 20:16). So if apostles are first, then apostles are also last.

Before Paul wrote "first apostles," he wrote 1 Corinthians 4:9: *"For I think that God has displayed us, **the apostles, last**, as men condemned to death; for we have been made a spectacle to the world, both to angels and to men"* (1 Cor. 4:9). Paul stated early in his letter that apostles were last, and later he mentions that apostles are first. So how do apostles become first? The answer is found in 1 Corinthians 4:9-13:

For it seems to me that God has put us apostles on display at the end of the procession, like those condemned to die in the arena. We have been made a spectacle to the whole universe, to angels as well as to human beings. We are fools for Christ, but you are so wise in Christ! We are weak, but you are strong! You are honored, we are dishonored! To this very hour we go hungry and thirsty, we are in rags, we are brutally treated, we are homeless. We work hard with our own hands. When we are cursed, we bless; when we are persecuted, we endure it; when we are slandered, we answer kindly. We have become the scum of the earth, the garbage of the world—right up to this moment. (1 Cor. 4:9-13)

Apostles serve the most and are treated the worst; they are the *"scum of the earth, the garbage of the world."* So, in 1 Corinthians 4, Paul talks about apostles being last and treated the absolute worst, then in 1 Corinthians 12:28 he says apostles are first. Let's look closer at the context in chapter twelve to see what Paul was saying:

Just as a body, though one, has many parts, but all its many parts form one body, so it is with Christ. For we were all baptized by one Spirit so as to form one body—whether Jews or Gentiles, slave or free—and we were all given the one Spirit to drink. Even so the body is not made up of one part but of many.

Now if the foot should say, "Because I am not a hand, I do not belong to the body," it would not for that reason stop being part of the body. And if the ear should say, "Because I am not an eye, I do not belong to the body," it would not for that reason stop being part of the body. If the whole body were an eye, where would the sense of hearing be? If the whole body were an ear, where would the sense of smell be? But in fact God has placed the parts in the body, every one of them, just as he wanted them to be. If they were all one part, where would the body be? As it is, there are many parts, but one body.

The eye cannot say to the hand, "I don't need you!" And the head cannot say to the feet, "I don't need you!" **On the contrary, those parts of the body that seem to be weaker are indispensable, and the parts that we think are less honorable we treat with special honor. And the parts that are unpresentable are treated with special modesty, while our presentable parts need no special treatment. But God has put the body together, giving greater honor to the parts that lacked it,** *so that there should be no division in the body, but that its parts should have equal concern for each other. If one part suffers, every part suffers with it; if one part is honored, every part rejoices with it.*

Now you are the body of Christ, and each one of you is a part of it. And God has placed in the church first of all apostles, *second prophets, third teachers, then miracles, then gifts of healing, of helping, of guidance, and of different kinds of tongues.* (1 Cor. 12:12-28)

In this passage, Paul is saying that every part of the body matters, that we are each unique and serve different purposes, and that we should honor each other. This is a true summary. Yet we typically miss Paul's deeper point about the dishonorable body parts and special modesty.

Compare these two passages:

. . . and the parts that we think are less honorable we treat with special honor. (1 Cor. 12:23a)

We are fools for Christ, but you are so wise in Christ! We are weak, but you are strong! **You are honored, we are dishonored!** *To this very hour we go hungry and thirsty, we are in rags, we are brutally treated, we are homeless.* (1 Cor. 4:10-11)

Paul is talking about apostles in both passages. He is saying that apostles (and by extension, fivefold ministers) are the dishonorable parts of the body and that the dishonorable parts of the human body are treated with special care and modesty. Paul is actually being a little bit crude here; he is saying that the fivefold ministry represents *the reproductive* and *excretory systems* of the body. Read the passage again:

> **On the contrary, those parts of the body that seem to be weaker are indispensable, and the parts that we think are less honorable we treat with special honor. And the parts that are unpresentable are treated with special modesty, while our presentable parts need no special treatment. But God has put the body together, giving greater honor to the parts that lacked it** *so that there should be no division in the body, but that its parts should have equal concern for each other. If one part suffers, every part suffers with it; if one part is honored, every part rejoices with it.*
>
> **Now you are the body of Christ, and each one of you is a part of it. And God has placed in the church first of all apostles,** *second prophets, third teachers, then miracles, then gifts of healing, of helping, of guidance, and of different kinds of tongues.* (1 Cor. 12:22-28)

The fivefold ministry deserves special honor in the body of Christ, because they are the dishonorable parts of the body of Christ. They are not the big muscles, or the neck, or the eyes, or the hands. Nope, they are the reproductive and excretory systems of the body. They are here to serve—to be ignored and unacknowledged.

Without an excretory system, the body becomes toxic, and without reproduction, humanity would die out. Therefore, the church should treat them with special honor, not because of position, title, or authority, but because of their down-and-dirty, humble, foot-washing service to the body of Christ. They should be honored the most because they serve the hardest.

Apostles are first, because their service is more dishonored than prophets. Prophets deserve the place of second honor because their service is more dirty and brutal than the teachers who are third. This isn't about positional authority. Whoever is last is going to be first. It's about service creating a spot in first place, based solely on honor for one's service.

THREE CHARACTERISTICS OF FIVEFOLD LEADERS

Over the last two decades, many in the church have begun to understand Ephesians 4:11–13 in a new light:

> *So Christ himself gave the apostles, the prophets, the evangelists,*
> *the pastors and teachers, to equip his people for works of service,*
> *so that the body of Christ may be built up until we all reach unity*
> *in the faith and in the knowledge of the Son of God and become*
> *mature, attaining to the whole measure of the fullness of Christ.*

Emerging teaching on these verses has done a lot to restore the fivefold ministry of apostles, prophets, evangelists, pastors, and teachers to the body of Christ. According to what Paul wrote in Ephesians 4, these fivefold ministers exist to equip the body of Christ. This purpose has been the primary message of those who teach on the fivefold ministry, and I completely agree with it.

What I'd like to add to this is an examination of what it really means to be equippers (leaders) in the church. A clearer understanding of fivefold identity will also help to equip the equippers. Jesus told us that leading in the church looks different than it does in the world. The question is, how? In what ways does it look different?

If we ask ourselves, practically speaking, what it looks like to be an equipper, what images come to our minds? Do they involve fame and power, or the opportunity to serve? Too often, I believe we in the church have viewed leadership as more akin to stardom than servanthood. Yet the reality of the role of an equipper—someone who trains others and leads them into maturity—inherently contains the idea of service. Like a good parent, a leader equips his or her followers through service, safety, and affection. These are the marks of the new covenant leaders who are emerging in the body of Christ. Such leaders do not use their authority to monopolize power and create an atmosphere of rules and fear. That is the world's way of leading. Instead, new covenant leaders lead a lot like Jesus:

1. They exhibit servant-hearted authority in humility.
2. They create environments where people can be vulnerable and transparent.
3. They are affectionate and warm.

In short, they bring healthy family life to church and truly equip disciples instead of indoctrinating followers. In the next three sections, I will examine each of these Jesus-style leadership methods in detail.

SERVANT-HEARTED

In their early years, Jesus' disciples vied and connived in an attempt to gain power. The power-seeking undercurrents among the twelve surfaced when James and John, the sons of Zebedee, brought their mother to Jesus with a special request. She said to Him, *"Grant that one of these two sons of mine may sit at your right and the other at your left in your kingdom"* (Matt. 20:21). It was a classic attempt at political maneuvering, but Jesus would have none of it.

He said to the two brothers, who were standing with their mother, hoping to be promised positions of power in Jesus' coming reign: *"You don't know what you are asking. . . . Can you drink the cup I am going to drink?"* (Matt. 20:22).

Not surprisingly, the other ten disciples responded in anger when they discovered the brothers' scheme. To avoid an all-out brawl, Jesus called a family meeting. It was time for Leadership 101. He said:

You know that the rulers of the Gentiles lord it over them, and their high officials exercise authority over them. Not so with you. Instead, whoever wants to become great among you must be your servant, and whoever wants to be first must be your slave—just as the Son of Man did not come to be served, but to serve, and to give his life as a ransom for many. (Matt. 20:25–28)

In response to their jockeying for position, Jesus told them they were acting just like all the power-hungry leaders in the world, and He called them out, saying, *"Not so with you."* This is not how His disciples act.

It's important to recognize what Jesus was saying *no* to here—and what He wasn't. While He rebuked the disciples' power-hungry attitudes, He did not censure their desire for greatness. He didn't tell them they shouldn't want to be great. He just redefined what greatness looks like. They'd grown up (like many of us) equating greatness with power and fame—with the ability to get what one wants. That was the dominant view, but Jesus (as He loved to do) called the standard into question. His formula for greatness probably seemed like the opposite of greatness to His disciples. And it begs the question: What is true greatness?

Our definition of greatness is often based on what Jesus called "the leaven of Herod." Using a metaphor based on a common activity of His day—the baking of bread using leaven, or yeast—Jesus had already told His disciples to avoid both the leaven of Herod and the leaven of the Pharisees (see Mark 8:15). Instead, He promised the leaven of the kingdom would work its way through the whole loaf (see Matt. 13:33).

The leaven of the Pharisees is the religious system. This system attempts to make everything look right and demands everything is done perfectly. By contrast, the leaven of Herod is the political system, which manifests in having power over other people. It is a desire for power and for control. These two systems (the leaven of the Pharisees and Herod) directly contradict the standard of the kingdom of God, which is built on a bottom-up, servant-based authority.

Jesus was that type of leader: the kingdom-of-God kind. He did not come to overpower or condemn or judge the world (see John 12:47). Instead, as He told His disciples, He came to serve and to give His life as a ransom for many. Jesus had modeled this so well for His disciples, but they were still clueless. Their minds had not yet been renewed to understand the reality of greatness in the kingdom.

Many of us also need our minds renewed on this subject. Even as we pursue the kingdom of God, we can get derailed by the leaven of the Pharisees (becoming legalistic and religious) or the leaven of Herod (becoming power-hungry and controlling). We think things like: "If we can take over a certain realm of society, then we can fix it." Accordingly, we move into a controlling spirit in our desire to "take over." The desire for necessary change is good, but the method we've adopted does not belong in the kingdom. Instead, we need to understand greatness the way Jesus defined and exemplified it for us.

Jesus gave His disciples another lesson on greatness when He told them:

> *Unless you change and become like little children, you will never enter the kingdom of heaven. Therefore, whoever takes the lowly*

position of this child is the greatest in the kingdom of heaven. (Matt. 18:3–4)

Once again, Jesus made it clear that He has no problem with a desire for greatness. But He changed it up again when He held up children as the standard. In His day, society valued children much less than it does today. Considering a child's almost absolute lack of rights or power—what Jesus called the "lowly position"—His statement must have been both terrifying and mystifying to His disciples. How could one possibly associate greatness in the kingdom with the position of a child? The disciples' grid for greatness was very far from His.

Clearly, if we want to be Jesus-style leaders, we need to understand greatness from His perspective. While we see this perspective most powerfully in Jesus' ultimate act of kingdom-style greatness—His sacrificial death on the cross—we also see it in His great demonstration of servant leadership in the last hours before His death. At the Last Supper, Jesus chose to demonstrate servant-based authority to His disciples one final time. It was that important to Him. He knew they needed to get it. The Bible describes Jesus' motive this way: *"Having loved his own who were in the world, he now showed them the full extent of his love"* (John 13:1). This was no insignificant matter. The passage goes on to say:

Jesus knew that the Father had put all things under his power, and that he had come from God and was returning to God. (John 13:3)

Jesus possessed unlimited power, and He knew it. He also knew where He had come from (identity) and where He was going (purpose). The apostle John tells us Jesus knew His own greatness and the scope of His authority even before the cross, and in light of these very great realities, He purposefully decided, yet again, to take the position of a servant. In other words, the power didn't go to His head. It only caused Him to bend lower and love more. This is why He got up in the middle of the Last Supper, took off His outer garments, and wrapped a towel around His waist so He could wash the disciples' feet.

Though He held the most amazing position possible as the all-powerful Son of God, Jesus humbled Himself in a very tangible way. It's like Pope Francis washing and kissing the feet of refugees, as he did during Holy Week in 2016, only to a far greater degree. Imagine becoming the president, king, or top leader of the largest nation or organization in the world. Jesus' position far exceeded any of those. God had given Him *all* power. It is hard to even comprehend the meaning of such a grand declaration. As Jesus stood in that incredible moment, the natural conclusion for Him was, "This means I need to wash some feet." It is almost incomprehensible for us, because it falls so far outside our grid for greatness. How in the world does that action make any sense to us?

Really, it *should* stun us. After all, foot-washing in that day was very different from foot-washing as we know it today. It is not too difficult to wash the reasonably clean feet of someone who showered that same morning and has been wearing socks and shoes all day. In Jesus' day, such foot cleanliness did not exist. People wore open-toed sandals and walked on dirt roads behind camels in a very warm climate, making foot-washing a messy job assigned to the lowest slave in the house. It was the lowest of low positions to be the one who cleaned dirt and sweat and "camel stuff" off people's feet when they entered a home.

Yet *that* is what Jesus did! When Jesus talked about leadership, He meant that those who are the greatest and have all of the power—those who are the most spiritual and have the greatest grace and calling—should willingly take the lowest place of servanthood in the house. Jesus' view was this: "Since God has given me the highest place, I need to take the lowest place." That's what leaders with great authority do; they take the lowest place of service. This is both natural and logical in the kingdom. Being a great leader means being the foot-washer.

This idea offended Peter (and probably the others, too). They were so convinced great leaders should be served that, to them, Jesus' decision to serve with such a humble task was a contradiction and offense to His greatness. Peter was probably thinking something along the lines of, "Jesus, you are the anointed big shot. You shouldn't be washing feet." Because his understanding was informed by the leaven of Herod, or the political system, he thought it was only right for leaders to "lord it over" their people (see Matt. 20:25).

Therefore, when Jesus got to Peter, Peter actually refused to let Him wash His feet. Jesus, ever patient, said, *"You do not realize now what I am doing, but later you will understand"* (John 13:7). But Peter still refused, saying, *"You shall never wash my feet"* (John 13:8). Clearly, he felt very strongly about his leadership paradigm.

But so did Jesus, and He was unwilling to leave the future leaders of His church with a wrong understanding of authority. So He gave Peter an ultimatum: *"Unless I wash you, you have no part with me"* (John 13:8).

It is easy for us to miss how extreme and severe this statement was. We often think of Jesus' earlier rebuke of Peter—when He says, *"Get behind me, Satan!"* (Matt. 16:23)—as being harsher. But this was far worse. In that earlier rebuke, Jesus was saying, "You are thinking with the mind of man, not the mind of God." He was realigning Peter's thoughts. But here, Jesus was saying, "If you don't get this one thing I'm teaching you, you're out. If you don't get this, you don't understand the kingdom at all, and you don't get to be a leader in the kingdom. That's how foundational this is." This was so important to Jesus that He was willing to kick Peter off the team if he couldn't accept it. In other words, this is a really weighty issue, and we need to get it just as much as Peter did.

Fortunately, Peter quickly acquiesced, saying, *"Then, Lord...not just my feet but my hands and my head as well"* (John 13:9). Peter—always the one to run to extremes—goes right from flat-out refusal to imploring Jesus to wash him head-to-toe.

Still Peter didn't fully understand. In response, Jesus said:

> *A person who has had a bath needs only to wash his feet; his whole body is clean. And you are clean . . .* (John 13:10)

Peter, in his enthusiasm, was in danger of missing the principle Jesus wanted to teach him. Jesus' point was not that Peter needed a bath because he stank. Rather, Jesus was demonstrating that this level of authority requires this level of serving. The greater the level of leadership, the greater the amount of service. He was reversing Peter's paradigm.

After Jesus finished washing all the disciples' feet, He dressed and returned to His seat. Then He summarized exactly what He had done when He took the lowest place and washed their feet:

> *Do you understand what I have done for you? . . . You call me "Teacher" and "Lord," and rightly so, for that is what I am. Now that I, your Lord and Teacher, have washed your feet, you also should wash one another's feet. I have set you an example that you should do as I have done for you. I tell you the truth, no servant is greater than his master, nor is a messenger greater than the one who sent him. Now that you know these things, you will be blessed if you do them.* (John 13:12–17)

In other words, He was telling them, "You are not greater than I. If I used my authority to serve, so should you." This is central to understanding kingdom leadership.

One reason so many of us have a hard time with this concept is the prevailing confusion in the church regarding the words *authority* and *control*. Chances are, for those of us who have been in the church at least ten years, the word *authority* triggers us to think *control*. This is the model of authority much of the church gives us. We think of the pastor as the CEO of the church, the one who has ultimate decision-making power. We think, "If I have *this* much authority, then I have *this* much control over my environment and the people around me." A pastor of 100 has control over 100. This is the understanding of authority many of us have learned in the church, but it's not what Jesus taught.

He told His disciples the opposite: Authority is a responsibility to serve. In other words, if I have authority over 100 people, I have 200 feet to wash. After all, being given authority simply means being given a sphere of influence, and the proper way to use that influence (according to Jesus) is to serve.

Unfortunately, many of us have experienced controlling leadership at church, home, work, or some other place. These controlling environments are often very painful and damaging, and many people live with scars from these experiences for years. The bottom line is, people who confuse *authority* and *control* end up injuring other people, even if unintentionally. That is because they are leading the wrong way. They are misusing their responsibility to serve those they lead, and they are distorting authority into the ability to control. People are given authority to serve. In other words, when promotion to greater levels of authority comes in our lives, it means God trusts us to serve more people.

To many of us, this may sound really great, but we have a hard time comprehending its implications. We are so wired to think authority equals control that we have no grid for what servant authority would look like. What is the difference between *control* and *authority*? How does one have *authority* without having *control*, and what does that even mean?

In a nutshell, *control* is an imitation of *authority* that comes from fear and insecurity; it is a counterfeit authority. Control is not actual authority, but a fear-based reaction people operate in because they are trying to control their environment.[9] This is true of many leaders, but also of many individuals in their family and social relationships. The implication here is that the perceived need to have control, which so many of us feel, is a false need, and it is rooted in the fear of what will happen if we lose control. It is rooted in the fear of being hurt by people we can't control. When leaders lead with this foundation of self-protection through control, they are doing exactly what Jesus said we must not do.

Thankfully, the shift toward servant-based leadership is already happening in the church. New covenant leaders are rising to positions of authority with an understanding that their greatest privilege and calling is to serve. This is the kind of leadership Jesus washed feet for—the kind He gave His life for. As God in the flesh, He laid down His life as the foremost servant leader. Wherever He went, He loved the unlovely and washed the feet of His up-and-coming leaders saying, "Do this, or you have no part with me."

The truth is, being a leader is not all it's hyped up to be. It's less, and it's more. It's less about being famous, anointed, and full of deep revelation, and it's more about washing feet—even dirty feet. Yes, leaders equip the body of Christ, and that is important, but *most* important is that they lead like Jesus did, because servant leadership creates an environment of freedom and life. Only when we've served and loved people to life will our equipping settle in fertile soil.

---

[9] On this subject of control and freedom, I am deeply indebted to Danny Silk and his teachings on healthy relationships, especially in his books, *Loving Our Kids on Purpose* and *Culture of Honor*.

TRANSPARENT

Servant-based leadership creates freedom. And what does freedom do? It makes space for messes—even *big messes!* Remember, before Jesus washed His disciples' feet, they were all sitting together at dinner with dirty, stinky feet. Their mess was not hidden or controlled; it was obvious, which gave Jesus the chance to wash it clean.

Jesus loves to create opportunities for freedom. And for some reason unstated in the text, on that final climactic evening with His disciples, the usual servant who would have washed their feet as they arrived was absent. It was the perfect opportunity for Jesus to show them how a leader serves.

But it was also more than that. It was proof that God is not afraid of our messes. Under the old covenant, being unclean alienated people from God. Uncleanliness meant exclusion from the temple and corporate worship. Sometimes, if the uncleanness was permanent, it even meant living as an outcast. As a result, the law contained a long list of rules regarding what makes one unclean and how to become clean again. In Jesus' time, being clean was a very big deal. Probably, the disciples felt pretty self-conscious of their mess. Maybe they wondered what Jesus thought about it. Certainly, they never imagined *He* would wash their feet. They never imagined the Lord of all would be the one to come and make them clean.

But Jesus had come to introduce the new covenant and to show people what God is really like. He came to show us the face of a God who prioritizes freedom over control. And He came to invite us into the glorious possibilities that freedom holds.

Unfortunately, a lot of people incorrectly think God is controlling, which causes them to also be controlling. This is far from the truth. Instead, God finds honor and pleasure in having a bride (the church) He does *not* control—a bride who lives in great love and freedom and is capable of handling the authority He wants to give. In other words, He wants to be equally yoked with His church!

God didn't plan to redeem people so He could control them. That would be like a man rescuing a woman out of slavery and marrying her so he could control (enslave) her. If control is the basis of the relationship, what is the difference between the old master and the new? No, God had something different in mind. When Jesus used the metaphor of a bride and groom to describe His relationship with us, He meant it in the context of a healthy marriage between two free and loving people.

That is exactly why we need to walk as the glorious, bride without spot or wrinkle (see Eph. 5:27). Jesus does not want a bride who is the equivalent of a rude, petty thirteen-year-old girl who continually fights with others and causes issues. He longs for a mature bride— something He could only hope for in the context of freedom. We are not mature if we are dependent on having Him micromanage our every move. Maturity only comes through freedom—through having the ability to chose, to make mistakes, and to grow. That is exactly how Jesus led His disciples while on earth, and it's how He leads us today, too.

At the core of the gospel is this amazing truth: God is all about freedom—so much so, that wherever His Spirit is, He creates an environment of freedom (see 2 Cor. 3:17). The closer we get to Him, the more liberty we experience. Those who believe God is a controlling spirit think the closer we get to God, the more controlled the environment is. That is why many churches have so little freedom. But such a belief is rooted in a misunderstanding of God's nature and His desire for us. Does He want yes-men who do His bidding? Or does He want free partners with whom He can dream and create? Definitely the latter.

From the very beginning, God has demonstrated His value for freedom, sometimes at a very great cost to Himself. After all, He was the one who created the garden in Eden and decided to plant a forbidden tree in the middle of it! He didn't have to put that tree there, but He did because He values freedom, and He wanted humanity to always have a choice. He introduced a possibility for a bad decision because He knew we would not be truly free if we did not have the choice to disobey. In other words, we don't truly have freedom if we don't have a wrong option available. So God gave them a wrong option, not to mess with them but to give them a real choice, which created genuine freedom in their lives.

When we talk about such extravagant freedom, many of us are reminded of the apostle Paul's admonition that everything should be done *"in a fitting and orderly way"* (1 Cor. 14:40), or as the New King James Version puts it, *"decently and in order."* The problem is that we read "order" and think *control.* God's idea of order is often very different from ours. When He created the earth—including the garden of Eden and Adam and Eve—He pronounced it all good. In other words, He had made it according to His perfect order. It had all turned out exactly as He had wanted it. The existence of an opportunity for error did not negate that rightness or order.

In fact, considering what we've learned of God's value for freedom, we can safely say His definition of *"fitting and orderly"* always includes freedom (or the possibility of a bad choice). It does not mean a tight, rigid, and controlled environment. God loves to create opportunities for freedom, and sometimes those opportunities make us nervous because we still like to feel in control. It helps us feel safe, and when someone is overwhelmed by the power of God and falls on the floor in a church service, it might not feel very safe to us. But it is an opportunity for freedom, which means it is fitting and orderly.

The reason this feels so frightening to some of us is that an environment of freedom also allows people's dirt to come to the surface. Sometimes, that dirt can be downright stinky. But this, too, is according to God's divine order. He doesn't want us to live with our dirt and be stuck in destructive cycles; He wants to set us free so we can live in our destinies. In order for that to happen, we need a place where our issues can surface and people will love us through them to wholeness. Really, that's the essence of what it means to be a good leader—*to create an environment where people can find this kind of healing and begin to become who God created them to be.*

A controlling environment never produces free and healthy people, because people's issues are never allowed to surface. Instead, everyone lives trying to hide and protect their dirt, keeping it sheltered within them so no one sees it. They know that if the junk surfaces, they risk being stoned in the foyer. Religion creates an environment of fear and control, in which it is not okay to have problems. So often we are oblivious to what is really going on with people around us. And then one day we notice someone missing at church and ask around, only to find out, "Oh, didn't you hear? He had all of this stuff going on in his life that no one knew anything about, and last week he completely blew up his life when it all came out, and now he's gone." At those times, we wonder, "Why didn't he tell someone? Why couldn't he bring it to the surface?" He couldn't because the church wasn't a safe environment, and he was afraid of being ostracized or condemned. And that is a tragedy.

Of all places in this world, the church should be the safest. The church, like the Holy Spirit, should bring freedom. And if the Holy Spirit is at the center of what we do, He will help us do just that. That's what He does. He creates environments where people feel safe sharing their struggles, and then He helps them get free. This is what John meant when he wrote, *"If we walk in the light as He is in the light, we have fellowship with one another, and the blood of Jesus Christ His Son cleanses us from all sin"* (1 John 1:7). Freedom comes in safe environments with people who love and believe in us in the midst of our struggles and help us get cleaned up.

Freedom comes when you take off your shoes to reveal feet covered in camel stuff, and the leaders say, "Hey, it looks like you have a mess there. Let's wash your feet!" Good leaders will wash your dirty feet, not cut them off. They won't say, "Look at the problem you just brought in here. Look at what you did!" And they won't treat you in a way that brings shame or that seeks to control and manipulate you into compliance and acceptable behavior. That is not how the Holy Spirit works. Paul tells us, instead, that it is through God's kindness that He brings us to repentance (Rom. 2:4). And He wants His leaders to do the same.

The question is, how? How do we create an environment in which people feel truly safe and free to be themselves and let their issues surface? The apostle Paul faced this same question. In his second letter to the church of Corinth, which he had founded, he wrote:

We have spoken freely to you, Corinthians, and opened wide our hearts to you. We are not withholding our affection from you, but you are withholding yours from us. As a fair exchange—I speak as to my children—open wide your hearts also. (2 Cor. 6:11)

He wanted to create an environment of openness and freedom, but something was standing in the way. He wanted a fair exchange of life between them, so he urged them to open their hearts to him *just as he had already done toward them.* That is the key. Most people won't open their hearts just because a controlling leader tells them to. But that's not what was going on here. As Paul points out, he could ask the Corinthians to open their hearts to him as their leader, because he had already opened his heart to them. He was simply asking them to follow his example of openness and vulnerability.

When it comes to creating a free environment, leaders must set the example. As a leader, it is my job to open my heart to you first. Then, as a fair exchange, you should open your heart to me. The problem Paul faced was that, though he was not withholding his affection from the Corinthians, they were withholding theirs from him. The problem was on their side, and he invited them to reciprocate his example of vulnerability by opening themselves to him. It was not a manipulative command but a heart plea from a vulnerable position. It's important for us to see here that Paul did not wait to make sure it was "safe" for him to open his heart to them; no, he jumped in with wholehearted love, holding nothing back, despite the fact that these people might hurt or reject him.

That is the brave choice for openness and transparency that good leaders will make. And that choice makes all the difference in the environment a leader creates.

Unfortunately, a lot of people approach relationships with self-protection as a primary goal. When we live inside a system of control and think God is controlling, it is very easy to misunderstand the Bible. We read it through our worldview, and if our worldview is not biblical, we will misconstrue the meaning of Scripture. For example, the Bible says, *"Above all else, guard your heart, for everything you do flows from it"* (Prov. 4:23). A lot of people think this means we need to guard our hearts *from other people*. But that's not actually what the Bible says. We can know this for sure because it does not fit with the overarching message of sacrificial love in the Bible. God certainly didn't guard His heart from us. Why do we think He would want us to guard our hearts from others?

Instead of telling us to hold others at arm's length and guard ourselves *from* them, the Proverbs verse is saying we must guard our hearts because what we do flows *out* of our hearts. Or as the New King James Version puts it, *"out of it spring the issues of life."* In other words, we need to put a guard at our hearts to keep negative things from coming out and wounding others. This verse is all about the reality of how we affect the people around us through the attitude of our hearts. Guarding our hearts doesn't mean protecting our hearts from other people, but protecting other people from the overflow of our hearts. Jesus pointed out to His disciples that *"the mouth speaks what the heart is full of"* (Matt. 12:34). Similarly, in Hebrews 12:15 it speaks of how a bitter root (in the heart) will defile many if it is allowed to grow.

When we understand this, we also understand that this verse in Proverbs is telling us to keep watch over our hearts and to make sure that light and life are springing out of us—not bitterness or other negative emotions that create toxic environments and wound others. Really, this is all about being proactive in our love and care for our families, friends, and those we lead. It is about choosing to be the risk-takers who will guard the content of our hearts so we can overflow with open-hearted love and life toward all we meet. Simply put, guarding our hearts means being aware of what is in our hearts and making sure we don't defile others and create messes through our heart-overflow.

Jesus certainly didn't guard His heart *from* people. In fact, He took transparency even further. He didn't just give us His heart; He gave us His life. And He did it even though He knew many people would reject His love. Following Jesus means loving like He loved—sacrificially and with abandon. Leading like He leads means being the one to initiate transparency by opening our hearts first, even at the risk of being hurt. Jesus is our true standard for love and leadership, and He made open-hearted transparency a priority. This open-hearted transparency is essential to an environment in which people can feel free to allow their junk to surface. If authority without control is one half of the freedom puzzle, open-hearted transparency is the other.

By contrast, the natural result of a *lack* of transparency and an environment where people are *not* free to air their junk is a culture of suspicion. No one feels free to tell what's really going on with themselves, but everyone is making assumptions about what might be going on with others. The reason for this is the fear of man, which is rooted in legalism. The fear of man causes people to fear what others might think or say about them and whether or not they are "spiritual enough." This is the antithesis of transparency and open-heartedness.

In environments like this, people like to quote 1 Thessalonians

5:22, most often in the King James Version: *"Abstain from all appearance of evil."* If you grew up in the church, chances are that someone—at least once in your life—has told you to avoid the appearance of evil. The problem with that advice is that it creates a different application for every scenario, and it expands the list of "things to avoid" nearly to infinity.

Take, for example, the story of a friend of mine who grew up in Pennsylvania. Because she needed to avoid the appearance of evil, she was never allowed to park across the street from her church, even in the middle of huge snowstorms. Instead, she had to park three blocks away, in a public parking lot, and then walk to church—in rain and in snow. Across the street from her church were several parking spots that were always open on Sunday mornings, but they were off limits to her. Why? Because they were in front of a bar. And of course, she did not want to be seen getting out of her car in front of the bar. *What might someone think?* Instead, it was best to walk the three blocks in the snow and avoid the appearance of evil.

Here's the problem: 1 Thessalonians 5:22 doesn't actually mean we need to avoid all appearances of evil, and I can prove it—both through the Scripture and through Jesus' example.

Four hundred years ago, when the King James translation of the Bible was being written, the translators had two words to choose from when they translated the word *eidos*: "appearance" and "form." The original King James Version used "appearance," but all newer translations of the Bible, including the New King James, use the word "form." While these words do share similar meanings, their distinction is significant. The difference between avoiding all forms of evil (actual sin) and avoiding all appearances of evil (anything others could *construe* as sin) is massive. Clearly, the correct translation is "form." We are regularly told to avoid sin, but nowhere else in Scripture are we told to avoid things that might look like sin. (Unfortunately, the King James Version of the verse is still the most well known.) For some, this is a big mindset shift.

If this is not enough proof to debunk the idea of avoiding the appearance of evil, consider the life of Jesus, our model in all things. Jesus never seemed to worry about what others thought of His actions or the appearance of his actions. He had zero concern for anyone's suspicions about Him, even when He was accused of evil by the Pharisees (see Mark 2:16; Matt. 12:24). Sometimes, it almost seems as though He went out of His way to offend people's sensibilities. For example, in John 6, He preached in the synagogue:

Very truly I tell you, unless you eat the flesh of the Son of Man and drink his blood, you have no life in you. Whoever eats my flesh and drinks my blood has eternal life, and I will raise them up at the last day. For my flesh is real food and my blood is real drink. Whoever eats my flesh and drinks my blood remains in me, and I in them. Just as the living Father sent me and I live because of the Father, so the one who feeds on me will live because of me. (John 6:53–57)

Think about how confusing and offensive this must have been to His hearers. Afterward, discerning that His disciples were struggling to accept what He had said, Jesus told them:

Does this offend you? Then what if you see the Son of Man ascend to where he was before! The Spirit gives life; the flesh counts for nothing. The words I have spoken to you—they are full of the Spirit and life. Yet there are some of you who do not believe. (John 6:62–64)

He was not the least bit concerned that some might be offended and leave—to the point that He did not bother to explain what He meant, even to His disciples. As a result, many of His disciples stopped following Him (see John 6:66).

We are so used to reading Jesus' words that we can miss how shocking they sounded to their original hearers and how unconcerned He was with appearances. It is amazing how little He cared about people's opinions of Him and whether they understood Him or not. When Jesus said in John 8, *"Where I go, you cannot come,"* it is clear the people thought He meant He was going to kill Himself (see John 8:21–22). He was okay with giving people the impression He was suicidal. And He cared so little whether people understood what He was saying that He often spoke in very enigmatic and offensive metaphors. He was not bothered by anyone's confusion or suspicion or shock as He shredded the theology of the day.

When we consider the culture of suspicion rampant in the church today, this example of complete freedom from fear of man is powerful. Unfortunately, so many of us have grown up under the shadow of suspicion—not only living in fear of people's suspicions about us but also treating people according to our suspicions of them. This is a formula for how *not* to create a safe environment where people feel free to be transparent.

Consider, for example, what many American Christians would think if they saw a brother in Christ walking out of a bar. What would they assume about what he was doing there, and what would that cause them to do? Many of us would automatically think, *Oh no! I wonder if he's OK. Has he fallen? Is he depressed?* And we might spiral into all kinds of crazy suspicions about our brother and, in the process, agree with the accuser. We forget Paul told us not to regard others *"from a worldly point of view"* or *"according to the flesh"* (2 Cor. 5:16 NKJV). Paul said this in the context of a discussion about how believers spiritually die and are raised with Christ into a new and righteous nature. Because of this reality, we should not assume evil of them. Rather, we should assume good based on their new identity in Christ.

Who knows—maybe our friend who just walked out of the bar was ministering to the drunks inside, getting a bunch of people saved, healed, and delivered. Or maybe he was just catching up with an old friend over a drink and watching a game. But the spirit of religion wants us to go in the direction of suspicion and accusation. It causes us to see and assume what is wrong with people instead of seeing and believing the best. This ability to see the best in people is an attribute of love, which *"thinks no evil"* and *"believes all things"* (1 Cor. 13:5–6 NKJV). Love declares the best about people instead of looking for what's wrong with them.

Jesus' immunity to the fear of man and His refusal to be suspicious of others created a zone of freedom around Himself that allowed people's issues to come safely to the surface. Peter is a good example of creating such zones. He actually pulled Jesus aside and rebuked Him for saying He would die on the cross. What's most amazing about this is that Jesus had created an environment in which Peter felt free to do that. Peter wasn't worried he would be shunned and attacked. And though Jesus did rebuke Peter's words because he was wrong, He did not punish Peter for speaking his mind or having the wrong ideas. He set him straight and loved him through it.

Jesus had such a freedom zone around Him that, at one point, He even said of the disciples, *"How long shall I put up with you?"* (Mark 9:19). In other words, they weren't holding any of their issues back. Everything was out in the open. Jesus even put up with the request from James and John to call fire down on an unwelcoming Samaritan city during one of their ministry trips—*"just as Elisha did"* (John 9:54). This is unbelievably bad. Not only were they asking to kill people who didn't agree with them, they were specifically pointing their aggression at their racial enemies, the Samaritans. In response to their psychotic and racist request, which they felt completely free to make to Jesus, He rebuked them with these words:

You do not know what manner of spirit you are of. For the Son of Man did not come to destroy men's lives but to save them. (Luke 9:55–56)

Jesus didn't allow their issues to harm others, but He allowed them the freedom to make mistakes. And He didn't kick them off the team when they did. He didn't clamp down on His disciples to make sure they wouldn't misrepresent Him or do something the wrong way. Instead, He allowed them so much freedom that some of us think it was a little crazy. But amazingly, in that freedom zone Jesus created, people's issues could surface, and He could help them mature. People could be themselves around Him—issues and all. Then, grace could deal with their brokenness. So many leaders are afraid of that process because they don't want people's issues to get out of control. But the reality is that grace can't deal with issues that are never brought into the light. And people won't bring their issues into the light if they are not in a freedom zone where people love instead of control.

Servant leaders aren't worried about being the big shot, so they are able to live in freedom and be vulnerable and transparent with those they lead. They share their own mistakes so others will feel safe to share mistakes too. In such an environment, struggles can surface, and people will mature. This is exactly what we need in the church. We don't need to do "church" together; we need to do *life* together. We need to be real. Fivefold leaders are to set the example, not of perfection, but of open-hearted transparency.

AFFECTIONATE

In 1999, I started a Bible study in my living room with four other young people. When we outgrew that space, we found a local café that allowed us to hold our Bible study on their "quiet" night. So every Thursday night, around forty-five people showed up and took over pretty much every chair in the café. We started our time with worship, using music from CDs. One of the songs we played every week had a big drum intro, and we dubbed this song "the hugging song." That meant that when the drums started playing, we all had three-and-a-half minutes to try to hug everyone in the room before the song ended. It was glorious chaos.

As far as I knew, everyone loved it. Even the café baristas fought over the Thursday night shifts because they loved being part of what we were doing. When people walked in off the street to get coffee and got hugged by a bunch of very happy strangers, they were surprised but never upset. They would ask, "What is this? This is a *church*? What are you talking about?" At that time, being a goth was popular, and goths often came in and were surprised by the hugs, too. They would freak out and say things like, "This is *not* a church!"

Some of our regulars told me Thursday night was the only time they felt loved all week, because it was the only time anyone hugged them. No one else—not their parents, siblings, or friends—hugged them. Incredibly, many people began to experience this Bible study as a place of real family. They would say things like, "This is not like the institution I grew up in. This is a family, and I feel it!"

However, there was one person among us who did not like the hugging song—not at all. After a while, people started noticing that whenever the hugging song came on, this friend was nowhere to be found. We wondered, "Where did he go?" So we decided to keep an eye out for him. It wasn't long before we discovered that he would hide in the men's room every week during the hugging song.

"Hey man," I asked him one night. "What's going on? Are you uncomfortable? What's the issue?"

"Well," he said, "I just think of a hug as a very personal thing. I share it with family, and that's kind of where I want to keep it."

"Okay," I said, looking him in the eyes. "I understand that. Do you understand that we are family?"

He paused. "You know, I never once have thought of Christians as a family. Wow."

We both stood there a bit stunned—him by the reality of the

church being family, and me by the fact that he had never before experienced that reality.

That day was the beginning of something new for my friend. He began to choose to be more affectionate, and soon, the understanding and experience of church as family had completely revolutionized his heart. Now, all these years later, he continues to be one of my closest friends. And he no longer hides in the men's room when he sees a hug coming. In fact, he is one of the huggiest men I know.

It all started with the simple revelation that in the church, we are family. Real family. And affection is a normal and important part of a healthy family. If the kingdom of God is a family, which it is, then part of being a good leader means modeling the same level of warmth and affection that emotionally healthy family members use toward one another.

Church history holds a lot of confusion over what the kingdom of God really is. For example, during the Crusades, the kingdom of God was viewed as a political power, and as a result, Christians killed Muslims and tried to take over Jerusalem, thinking that was how the kingdom would come. More recently, the kingdom of God has been viewed as entirely a supernatural reality. Thus, the kingdom is manifested in bringing heaven to earth through healing, miracles, salvation, deliverance, and so forth. I agree with this definition of the kingdom, with a big addition—family. Ultimately, what exists in heaven is a family. Many times, the Bible tells us we are part of a family called the household of faith.

The apostle Paul used the language of a family to explain relationships within the body of Christ:

Do not rebuke an older man harshly, but exhort him as if he were your father. Treat younger men as brothers, older women as mothers, and younger women as sisters, with absolute purity. (1 Tim. 5:1–2)

He put every person in the church in the context of family. Whether man or woman, old or young, each one is part of the family. That is incredibly profound. The way we view the kingdom of God will determine how we operate within it. If we view it as an organization, we will act very differently than we will if we view it as a family. And that family perspective is vital when we talk about what it looks like to be a good leader in the kingdom.

Because the kingdom is a family, good leaders must be good fathers or mothers at home. After all, if they don't know how to lead a family well at home, they certainly won't be able to do it at church. Paul makes this very clear in his first letter to Timothy:

> *Here is a trustworthy saying: Whoever aspires to be an overseer desires a noble task. Now the overseer is to be above reproach, faithful to his wife, temperate, self-controlled, respectable, hospitable, able to teach, not given to drunkenness, not violent but gentle, not quarrelsome, not a lover of money. He must manage his own family well and see that his children obey him, and he must do so in a manner worthy of full respect. (If anyone does not know how to manage his own family, how can he take care of God's church?).* (1 Tim. 3:1–5)

Paul was saying, "How can you lead a church family if your own family stinks?" It makes sense. It's not harsh or legalistic; it's just a practical principle. It's logical. If a leader's children do not feel like their parents are there to serve, wash feet, and love with open-heartedness, transparency, and affection, then the simple and logical fact is that the leader isn't qualified to be a good leader in the church either. This, of course, doesn't exclude single people from leadership. We all have an opportunity to be family with those with whom we live and work closely. The point is, we can tell a lot about a leader's potential by looking at that person's family life and close associations.

Creating a family culture is an important key to Jesus-style leadership, and a very big part of this culture is godly affection. In my Bible study at the café, people began to feel like family and began to feel loved because I, their leader, led the way in affection. I treated others with healthy affection, and I created a space for everyone else to also be affectionate. As a result, the atmosphere of that café was a lot more like a big family reunion than a corporate meeting.

The Bible contains a lot of examples of the importance of warmth and affection in leadership (and in the Christian life in general), but culturally, we have tended to miss or gloss over these passages. Because of this, we've ended up with leadership principles that simply do not fit with how Jesus operated as a leader. And that is a problem.

The Bible was written in a Mediterranean context of affection. In Jesus' day, people commonly kissed others on the cheek as a greeting, and it was normal for Paul and Peter to encourage their readers to greet each other with a "holy kiss." Such affection is still normal today in many cultures. By contrast, the United States was founded by groups like the Pilgrims and Puritans, whose staunchly conservative religious ideals caused them to keep others at arm's length. Thus, a cultural chasm exists between what we see in Scripture and what most of us experience in North American churches.

If we want to lead like Jesus did, we need to side with the biblical example, regardless of culture. That doesn't necessarily mean we do everything the people in Jesus' time did in the same way. But it does mean we learn the importance of affection and warmth and apply it within our cultural context. The early church transformed their culture's reality of a greeting kiss into a "holy kiss" in the family of God. In our Western culture, communicating love would more likely look like a warm embrace.

It's helpful to understand that the early church didn't simply value the holy kiss as a cultural expression. The church was living under intense persecution, so when people gathered, they had a very real understanding that it could be the last time in this life they would see one another. Because of that, affection was a priority. For us, that mindset is hard to grasp because many of us go to the same church with mostly the same people for many years. We get used to seeing one another and because of comfortable familiarity, we sometimes lack motivation to really connect with others on a deep level. It is easier for us to think of the church as a club instead of a family if we are not enduring persecution together. We don't have external pressure pushing us together in that way.

I am not advocating for persecution. We can have churches that are like warm, free families regardless. Imagine how much more energizing and life-giving church would be if it looked like a big family. In a church that's a family, the leaders lead as loving parents who are there to serve, honor, lift up, equip, and wash feet. They live with vulnerable and transparent hearts toward all, helping people bring their real selves to the surface. As that happens, they embrace, love, and value people so fully that people truly feel valuable and loveable. They feel like sons and daughters who belong to a family and are surrounded by close family relationships. In this family context, people know who they are, and they know how they fit.

This powerful vision is the potential within the body of Christ. It is how God relates to us as our Father, and He has given us what we need to make this reality a daily experience with one another. This, I believe, is the foundational reality the church needs before we can begin to experience true unity. So many people talk about unity, but they haven't figured out family. As a result, their ideas of unity look like doctrinal agreement or citywide pastors' meetings. When people grudgingly meet together, though they don't like each other, simply because they want revival in their region, that is not unity. And it certainly isn't family either.

We will experience unity once we start living like family, once we start loving and valuing people so much that we stop fearing their differences and their issues. When we reach that place, unity will be easy. We need some hugging prophets to lead the way. We need some prophets like the Old Testament prophet Habakkuk, whose name actually means "embrace." When we lead the way in affection, we will restore the Father heart of God to the body, and that will be the beginning of real family happening in the church.

Jesus showed us exactly what this looks like (and what it doesn't look like, too) when He visited Simon the Pharisee's house. As He was reclining at the table, an immoral woman entered. She had heard Jesus was there, and she came to stand behind Him, weeping and wetting His feet with her tears. Then she wiped His feet with her hair and poured expensive perfume on them. We are so used to reading this story that many of us forget how incredibly awkward this would have been. It is little wonder that Simon the Pharisee was shocked by this display during his special dinner for Jesus. If we're honest, many of us would have struggled to appreciate it as well. But not Jesus.

When Simon thought to himself, *"If this man were a prophet, he would know who is touching him and what kind of woman she is— that she is a sinner"* (Luke 7:39), Jesus answered him, *"Simon, I have something to tell you"* (Luke 7:40). And Jesus told him a parable of two men who owed money to a moneylender. One owed him a small amount, and the other a large amount, but neither had the money to pay him back. So the moneylender decided to forgive both of their debts. Jesus asked Simon, *"Which of them will love him more?"* (Luke 7:42).

Simon guessed the one who had the bigger debt cancelled would love the moneylender more, and Jesus confirmed it, pointing to the woman as an example. He said:

Do you see this woman? I came into your house. You did not give me any water for my feet, but she wet my feet with her tears and wiped them with her hair. You did not give me a kiss, but this woman, from the time I entered, has not stopped kissing my feet. You did not put oil on my head, but she has poured perfume on my feet. Therefore, I tell you, her many sins have been forgiven—as her great love has shown. But whoever has been forgiven little loves little. (Luke 7:44–47)

Here Jesus gives a vivid contrast between Simon and the woman—and it was not at all the contrast Simon expected. Jesus pointed out the lack of warmth, affection, and service in Simon, who was a product of the religious establishment. Though it would have been normal—and even expected—in the culture at the time, Simon had not greeted Jesus with a kiss or offered Him water to wash and perfume for His feet. Amazingly, the woman did all three of these, even though it was not her responsibility in this setting. Simon, the leader of that house, should have stooped to serve by washing Jesus' feet. He should have offered Him perfume to remove any odor from walking in the heat and dust, and He should have greeted Him warmly with a kiss on the cheek. Simon didn't do these things because he carried the cold heart of religion.

For whatever reason, Simon had ignored these usual courtesies, and the woman of ill repute came in and performed them for Jesus instead. As she did, a real family interaction happened between the two of them. They participated in an actual exchange of kingdom love. Between that woman and the judgmental/cold-hearted religious institution, no love existed. She received no grace or understanding from them. But from Jesus, she received honor and value. As a respected teacher, Jesus could have thrown her out of the house and publicly shamed her, and everyone would have approved. He didn't have to let her cry upon, perfume, and kiss His feet. But He did.

He embraced her in the midst of her mess, and He imparted to her the grace she needed to find freedom and wholeness. He received her affection toward Him as pure, and He validated it before her critics. Because Jesus (unlike Simon) was free of the fear of man, He was not worried about what others might assume about Him because of this woman. And that enabled Him to love and lead her as a father—to welcome her into a family experience. This is the way the kingdom operates.

BOUNDARIES AND GRACES

Fivefold leaders have different boundaries and unique grace on their lives for those boundaries. They will get into your personal space in very different ways:

1. Prophets want to know if you are hearing from God, and if not, they will help you.

2. Evangelists want to know if you know Jesus, and if not, they will help you.

3. Pastors want to know about the health of your heart, mind, and relationships, and if needed, they will help you.

4. Teachers want to know the health of your thinking and perspectives, and if something is unhealthy, they will help you.

Then there are apostles. Apostles are focused on the other four and architecting the overall culture of the kingdom family and laying foundations. Apostles are typically challenging the boundaries of the other four.

- Apostles can disturb a prophet's boundaries by putting their feet on the ground and pushing them to be practical.

- Apostles can disturb an evangelist's boundaries by urging them to make disciples and not just converts.

- Apostles can disturb a pastor's boundaries by stirring up their comfortable nest and pushing congregations to live on the edge of kingdom reality.

- Apostles can disturb a teacher's boundaries by challenging them to move beyond theological theory to supernatural practice.[10]

We often think of the word "disturb" in a negative light. Yet if we continue to look at Jesus as our model, we'll see that He disturbed boundaries constantly—with a purpose: to equip people to advance the kingdom.

IN CONCLUSION

Healthy fivefold leadership is part of God's plan. Such leadership will be marked by its servant-heartedness, transparency, and affection. Fivefold ministers exist to equip the body of Christ, and we must understand their respective graces and callings for them to function together in the church for the kingdom of God.

---

[10] In response to these insights, many ask, "Who disturbs the apostle?" This is typically done by other apostles, such as Paul confronting Peter (Gal. 2:11) or the Jerusalem council gathering in Acts 15.

CHAPTER SIX

FALSE FIVEFOLD LEADERS

And I will keep on doing what I am doing in order to cut the ground from under those who want an opportunity to be considered equal with us in the things they boast about. **For such people are false apostles, deceitful workers, masquerading as apostles of Christ.** *And no wonder, for Satan himself masquerades as an angel of light. It is not surprising, then, if his servants also masquerade as servants of righteousness. Their end will be what their actions deserve.* (2 Cor. 11:12-15)

If God is bringing attention to true fivefold ministers in our day, then we should expect a surge of false fivefold ministers to appear. An important reminder is that people only counterfeit what is valuable. Nobody counterfeits pennies. So keep in mind that the fivefold is incredibly valuable, and that's why there has always been such an attack against it.

David Cannistraci wrote about all fivefold ministers having

counterfeits in his groundbreaking book, *Apostles and the Emerging Apostolic Movement.*[11] Here are the categories he gives:

False Prophets:

> *Watch out for false prophets. They come to you in sheep's clothing, but inwardly they are ferocious wolves.* (Matt. 7:15)

False Shepherds:

> *The thief comes only to steal and kill and destroy; I have come that they may have life, and have it to the full.*
>
> *I am the good shepherd. The good shepherd lays down his life for the sheep. The hired hand is not the shepherd and does not own the sheep. So when he sees the wolf coming, he abandons the sheep and runs away. Then the wolf attacks the flock and scatters it. The man runs away because he is a hired hand and cares nothing for the sheep.* (John 10:10-13)

False Teachers:

> *For the time will come when people will not put up with sound doctrine. Instead, to suit their own desires, they will gather around them a great number of teachers to say what their itching ears want to hear. They will turn their ears away from the truth and turn aside to myths.* (2 Tim. 4:3-4)

---

[11] David Cannistraci, *Apostles and the Emerging Apostolic Movement,* (Ventura, CA: Renew, 1996), 133.

But there were also false prophets among the people, just as there will be false teachers among you. They will secretly introduce destructive heresies, even denying the sovereign Lord who bought them—bringing swift destruction on themselves. (2 Peter 2:1)

False Evangelists:

As we have already said, so now I say again: If anybody is preaching to you a gospel other than what you accepted, let them be under God's curse! (Gal. 1:9)

False Apostles:

I know your deeds, your hard work and your perseverance. I know that you cannot tolerate wicked people, that you have tested those who claim to be apostles but are not, and have found them false. (Rev. 2:2)

Cannistraci goes on to write, "there are only two motives in Scripture for false leaders: Love of money (Titus 1:11; Rev. 2:14; 2 Peter 2:1-3; Jude 11) and Pride (1 Tim. 6:4-5)."[12]

They must be silenced, because they are disrupting whole households by teaching things they ought not to teach—and that for the sake of dishonest gain. (Titus 1:11)

Nevertheless, I have a few things against you: There are some among you who hold to the teaching of Balaam, who taught

---

[12] Cannistraci, *Apostles and the Emerging Apostolic Movement*, 135.

Balak to entice the Israelites to sin so that they ate food sacrificed to idols and committed sexual immorality. (Rev. 2:14)

But there were also false prophets among the people, just as there will be false teachers among you. They will secretly introduce destructive heresies, even denying the sovereign Lord who bought them—bringing swift destruction on themselves. Many will follow their depraved conduct and will bring the way of truth into disrepute. In their greed these teachers will exploit you with fabricated stories. Their condemnation has long been hanging over them, and their destruction has not been sleeping. (2 Peter 2:1-3)

Woe to them! They have taken the way of Cain; they have rushed for profit into Balaam's error; they have been destroyed in Korah's rebellion. (Jude 11)

. . . they are conceited and understand nothing. They have an unhealthy interest in controversies and quarrels about words that result in envy, strife, malicious talk, evil suspicions and constant friction between people of corrupt mind, who have been robbed of the truth and who think that godliness is a means to financial gain. (1 Tim. 6:4-5)

Jude calls these false leaders "clouds without rain" (Jude 12), which is to say that they look like they have substance, but they give no water, no life. They provide nothing useful. *"These people are blemishes at your love feasts, eating with you without the slightest qualm—shepherds who feed only themselves. They are clouds without rain, blown along by the wind; autumn trees, without fruit and uprooted—twice dead"* (Jude 12).

In the first century, these false apostles apparently weren't even operating in the supernatural. *"I persevered in demonstrating among you the marks of a true apostle, including signs, wonders and miracles"* (2 Cor. 12:12).

I have observed that the more controlling a leader is, the less the Holy Spirit or the supernatural will be in operation. *"Now the Lord is the Spirit, and where the Spirit of the Lord is, there is freedom"* (2 Cor. 3:17).

THE SUPER APOSTLES

In Corinth, Paul had to deal with a group of false apostles, to whom he gave a sarcastic nickname of "super-apostles":

> *I do not think I am in the least inferior to those "super-apostles."* (2 Cor. 11:5)

> *I have made a fool of myself, but you drove me to it. I ought to have been commended by you, for I am not in the least inferior to the "super-apostles," even though I am nothing.* (2 Cor. 12:11)

These super-apostles were arrogant, money-hungry control freaks:

> *You gladly put up with fools since you are so wise! In fact, you even put up with anyone who **enslaves you** or **exploits you** or **takes advantage of you** or **puts on airs** or **slaps you in the face.** To my shame I admit that we were too weak for that! Whatever anyone else dares to boast about—I am speaking as a fool—I also dare to boast about.* (2 Cor. 11:19-21)

The whole chapters of 2 Corinthians 11 and 12 are about Paul's contention with these usurpers. For the sake of review, let's look at 2 Corinthians 11 and see how Paul was dealing with them:

I hope you will put up with me in a little foolishness. Yes, please put up with me! I am jealous for you with a godly jealousy. I promised you to one husband, to Christ, so that I might present you as a pure virgin to him. But I am afraid that just as Eve was deceived by the serpent's cunning, your minds may somehow be led astray from your sincere and pure devotion to Christ. For if someone comes to you and preaches a Jesus other than the Jesus we preached, or if you receive a different spirit from the Spirit you received, or a different gospel from the one you accepted, you put up with it easily enough.

I do not think I am in the least inferior to those "super-apostles." I may indeed be untrained as a speaker, but I do have knowledge. We have made this perfectly clear to you in every way. Was it a sin for me to lower myself in order to elevate you by preaching the gospel of God to you free of charge? I robbed other churches by receiving support from them so as to serve you. And when I was with you and needed something, I was not a burden to anyone, for the brothers who came from Macedonia supplied what I needed. I have kept myself from being a burden to you in any way, and will continue to do so. As surely as the truth of Christ is in me, nobody in the regions of Achaia will stop this boasting of mine. Why? Because I do not love you? God knows I do!

And I will keep on doing what I am doing in order to cut the ground from under those who want an opportunity to be considered equal with us in the things they boast about. For such people are false apostles, deceitful workers, masquerading as apostles of Christ. And no wonder, for Satan himself masquerades as an angel of light. It is not surprising, then, if his servants also masquerade as servants of righteousness. Their end will be what their actions deserve.

I repeat: Let no one take me for a fool. But if you do, then tolerate me just as you would a fool, so that I may do a little boasting. In this self-confident boasting I am not talking as the Lord would, but as a fool. Since many are boasting in the way the world does, I too will boast. You gladly put up with fools since you are so wise! In fact, you even put up with anyone who enslaves you or exploits you or takes advantage of you or puts on airs or slaps you in the face. To my shame I admit that we were too weak for that!

Whatever anyone else dares to boast about—I am speaking as a fool—I also dare to boast about. Are they Hebrews? So am I. Are they Israelites? So am I. Are they Abraham's descendants? So am I. Are they servants of Christ? (I am out of my mind to talk like this.) I am more. I have worked much harder, been in prison more frequently, been flogged more severely, and been exposed to death again and again. Five times I received from the Jews the forty lashes minus one. Three times I was beaten with rods, once I was pelted with stones, three times I was shipwrecked, I spent a night and a day in the open sea, I have been constantly on the move. I have been in danger from rivers, in danger from bandits, in danger from my fellow Jews, in danger from Gentiles; in danger in the city, in danger in the country, in danger at sea; and in danger from false believers. I have labored and toiled and have often gone without sleep; I have known hunger and thirst and have often gone without food; I have been cold and naked. Besides everything else, I face daily the pressure of my concern for all the churches. Who is weak, and I do not feel weak? Who is led into sin, and I do not inwardly burn?

If I must boast, I will boast of the things that show my weakness. The God and Father of the Lord Jesus, who is to be praised forever, knows that I am not lying. In Damascus the governor under King Aretas had the city of the Damascenes guarded in order to arrest me. But I was lowered in a basket from a window in the wall and slipped through his hands. (2 Cor. 11)

Paul points to his willingness to suffer for the gospel, his love for the churches, the fact that when people walk in sin it affected his heart, his jealousy for God's people, and his humility. These are the traits of true apostles.

NICOLAITANS

Corinth wasn't the only place struggling with false fivefold leaders. We know that Ephesus also had a similar problem. Paul actually warned them in Acts 20 that these false leaders were coming:

> *Keep watch over yourselves and all the flock of which the Holy Spirit has made you overseers. Be shepherds of the church of God, which he bought with his own blood. I know that after I leave, savage wolves will come in among you and will not spare the flock. Even from your own number men will arise and distort the truth in order to draw away disciples after them. So be on your guard! Remember that for three years I never stopped warning each of you night and day with tears.* (Acts 20:28-31)

By the time we get to the apostle John writing the book of Revelation, we see that these false leaders had tried to infiltrate the Ephesian church:

> *But you have this in your favor: You hate the practices of the Nicolaitans, which I also hate.* (Rev. 2:6)

The mystery of the Nicolaitans is a fascinating one. We have very little historical information to tell us who they were and what God hated about them. According to Irenaeus, the Nicolaitans were founded by Nicolas, the proselyte of Antioch, who was one of the seven deacons chosen to serve at the tables in Acts 6:5:

> *This proposal pleased the whole group. They chose Stephen, a man full of faith and of the Holy Spirit; also Philip, Procorus, Nicanor, Timon, Parmenas, and Nicolas from Antioch, a convert to Judaism* (Acts 6:5).

This Nicolas started as a pagan, converted to Judaism, and then converted to Christianity. He was chosen to serve as a deacon, but then, according to Irenaeus, he apostatized. He walked away from Christianity and started a movement called the Nicolaitans.

We do not know for sure what the Nicolaitans taught, but their name means "conqueror of the laity" or "conqueror of the people." Thus, it would seem that their heresy related to church government. As I noted in my book, *Understanding the Seven Churches of Revelation*, David Chilton and Watchman Nee both agree that the Nicolaitan heresy had something to do with hierarchical control of other people.[13] Nee wrote, "Nicolaitans, then, refers to a group of people who esteem themselves higher than the common believers." And Chilton shares that the word for Nicolaitans is *ivik-ohzos* in Greek, which means "conqueror of the people."

The man who had converted from paganism to Judaism to Christianity—and who had been given a position to serve— eventually became a dominator of people. He fell from being a servant-hearted man to starting a movement based on power and control over others. It is a tragic story.

Though the Nicolaitan heresy flourished in some churches (as we will see next, in Pergamum), in Ephesus it was soundly squelched.

---

[13] See page 60.

Perhaps this is because the apostle Paul had spent so much time teaching the Ephesians what the kingdom of God is like.

In his letter to the Ephesians, we read Paul's command to mutually submit to one another: *"Submit to one another out of reverence for Christ"* (Eph. 5:21). And when Paul laid out the fivefold leadership of the church, he taught that the role of apostles, prophets, evangelists, pastors, and teachers is for serving and equipping other believers (see Eph. 4:11–13), not for controlling them.

In Ephesus, Paul laid a foundation for servant-hearted leadership—not hierarchy and domineering leadership. Because of this, the Ephesians hated the Nicolaitan control and abuse just as much as God did.

PERGAMUM: THE ROMAN CAPITAL

> *"Nevertheless, I have a few things against you: There are some among you who hold to the teaching of Balaam, who taught Balak to entice the Israelites to sin so that they ate food sacrificed to idols and committed sexual immorality. Likewise, you also have those who hold to the teaching of the Nicolaitans."* (Rev. 2:14-15)

Unlike the believers at Ephesus, who rejected the Nicolaitan teaching, some of the Pergamum believers were following these false teachings related to authority and control. Considering that Pergamum was the government's capital and a military city, it is not surprising that the believers there would have been tempted to take their cues from secular leaders and *"lord it over"* each other (Matt. 20:25). But Jesus made it clear that He does not endorse that type of leadership. Again, when His disciples jockeyed for position, He told them:

. . . whoever wants to become great among you must be your servant, and whoever wants to be first must be your slave—just as the Son of Man did not come to be served, but to serve, and to give his life as a ransom for many. (Matt. 20:26-28)

Instead of dominating the people, the leaders of His church should be gentle shepherds like Him, as the apostle Peter explains:

Be shepherds of God's flock that is under your care, watching over them—not because you must, but because you are willing, as God wants you to be; not pursuing dishonest gain, but eager to serve; not lording it over those entrusted to you, but being examples to the flock. (1 Peter 5:2-3)

Jesus, the servant-hearted Great Shepherd, hates controlling and authoritarian leadership. Seeing that some of the believers in Pergamum were creating an oppressive hierarchy and seeking to dominate the people, He gives them an ultimatum:

Repent therefore! Otherwise, I will soon come to you and will fight against them with the sword of my mouth. (Rev. 2:16)

In this verse, we see a division among the people. Jesus says, I will come to *you*, and I will fight against *them*. He is going to come to the church at Pergamum, and He is going to fight against those holding to the teaching of the Nicolaitans. This is why He changes the pronoun from *you* to *them*. His fight is not with the entire church, but with those following this heresy. Gordon Fee sums it up like this:

[14] Gordon Fee, *Revelation*, (Eugene, OR: Cascade Books, 2011), 35.

This is not a battle against the whole church, although they are indeed to repent for letting this false teaching exist among them, but warfare carried on specifically "against them", the purveyors of and adherents to this false teaching.[14]

At the beginning of the letter, Jesus introduces Himself as the one with the double-edged sword—the one who has true authority. Here, in response to the abuse of authority, He threatens to use that sword.

Here are three rules to follow when you encounter controlling, false leaders:

1. Avoid them:

I urge you, brothers and sisters, to watch out for those who cause divisions and put obstacles in your way that are contrary to the teaching you have learned. Keep away from them. (Rom. 16:17)

But avoid foolish controversies and genealogies and arguments and quarrels about the law, because these are unprofitable and useless. Warn a divisive person once, and then warn them a second time. After that, have nothing to do with them. You may be sure that such people are warped and sinful; they are self-condemned. (Titus 3:9-11)

. . . and constant friction between people of corrupt mind, who have been robbed of the truth and who think that godliness is a means to financial gain. (1 Tim. 6:5)

2. Don't submit to them:

This matter arose because some false believers had infiltrated our ranks to spy on the freedom we have in Christ Jesus and to make us slaves. We did not give in to them for a moment, so that the truth of the gospel might be preserved for you. (Gal. 2:4-5)

3. Teach the opposite:

He must hold firmly to the trustworthy message as it has been taught, so that he can encourage others by sound doctrine and refute those who oppose it. (Titus 1:9)

We have looked at the false fivefold movement inside the New Testament, but let us remember that Paul's answer to the false fivefold was to actually have the true fivefold leaders in place. They keep us from being tossed about by every wind of doctrine:

So Christ himself gave the apostles, the prophets, the evangelists, the pastors and teachers, to equip his people for works of service, so that the body of Christ may be built up until we all reach unity in the faith and in the knowledge of the Son of God and become mature, attaining to the whole measure of the fullness of Christ.

Then we will no longer be infants, tossed back and forth by the waves, and blown here and there by every wind of teaching and by the cunning and craftiness of people in their deceitful scheming. (Eph. 4:11-14)

As I mentioned at the start of this chapter, people only counterfeit what is valuable. The fact that there are false fivefold indicates the importance of the *true* fivefold. When you encounter what is false, avoid it, don't submit to it, and teach the opposite—the truth.

CHAPTER SEVEN

THE RESIDUE OF THE SHEPHERDING MOVEMENT

In the United States in the 1970s, an incredibly influential movement arose which continues to have a residual effect to this day. I am referring to the Shepherding Movement (also called the Fathering or Discipleship Movement).[15] This was originally established to bring health and accountability to leaders so that they wouldn't work in isolation and fall apart in ministry. Yet it developed into a very toxic hierarchical structure of government and control. Many books have been written detailing the movement's history and outcomes, and I highly recommend reading *The Shepherding Movement* by S. David Moore.[16] Moore was not actually injured by

[15] In my research on the fivefold, I found that after the Shepherding Movement of the 1970s, a second movement of fivefold restoration took place between 1995-2005 under apostle C. Peter Wagner, known as the New Apostolic Reformation. This brought a wave of books on the topic of fivefold to the body of Christ. But from 2006-2016, almost nothing new or revelatory was published or pioneered (with a few exceptions). It is my wholehearted desire that this book triggers a third wave of understanding and the actual implementation of the fivefold in local congregations happens at long last!

[15] S. David Moore, *The Shepherding Movement: Controversy and Charismatic Ecclesiology* (New York, NY: T&T Clark International, 2003).

the movement, so he is able to write without a wounded bias, while being very honest and factual.

Rather than rehashing the movement's mistakes, I want to address one of the main root causes that opened the door to many other mistakes. The catalysts of this movement drew from the governmental stories of Moses and David in the Old Testament, creating an application of spiritual authority that led to a lot of authoritarian abuse and control.

Here is the bottom line: your pastor is not King Saul, and you are not young David. Your pastor is not Moses, and you are not Korah. Can we learn from these stories? Yes. But are these stories the models of how church government is meant to function—or are they the recorded history of how theocracies and monarchies functioned in the Old Testament? Shouldn't we be looking at Jesus and the disciples to understand new covenant leadership?

In his book, *God's Leaders for Tomorrow's World*, Harold Eberle wrote a brilliant piece about understanding the four lines of authority:

Authority structure pervades everything in this world. If it were not for authority, you would not know on which side of the road to drive your car, or whether or not you should stop at the red light. Your car never would have been made at a factory, because people cannot be organized to work together without a leadership structure. The home in which you live is established and protected by authority. Not only is your home protected from enemies of another country, but neither can your neighbor simply walk in without your permission. The grocery store in which you shop is dependent upon authority to carry on its daily activities; otherwise, employees would not know what to do and customers simply could walk out the door with merchandise. Everything you do throughout the day is permeated by authority structures.

The Bible shows us four distinct lines of authority in the world: the government, the Church, the family, and the individual. Each of these entities is responsible before God. Let's examine each of these.

In Romans, Chapter 13, we find clear instructions about how we should recognize the authority of the established government. The Apostle Paul wrote:

Let every person be in subjection to the governing authorities. For there is no authority except from God, and those, which exist are established by God (Rom. 13:1).

The context of this verse is leaders who govern society. This government does not include merely political leaders, but all authority that is delegated to establish civil order. This extends all the way from the king or president down to the local community, business, or school. God is behind such leadership. Of course, not all natural governmental systems are upholding godly principles, but we—as Bible-believers—must acknowledge that God Himself is the One who establishes governmental order.

The second line of authority is the Church. God gives clear instructions in the New Testament about the function and roles of elders and all leaders within the Church. Several Bible verses speak about authority and submission within the Body of Christ (i.e., I Peter 5:5). Christians are exhorted:

Obey your leaders, and submit to them; for they keep watch over your souls, as those who will give an account. (Heb. 13:17)

Submission is a meaningless word apart from authority. This authority is from God and we are told that the leaders will be held accountable to God.

Third is the authority, which God has ordained for the family unit. The father is the head of his family (I Cor. 11:3), a husband and wife are called to rule together, and the children are to obey their parents (Eph. 6:1-2). So important is it for children to honor their parents that it was recorded as one of the Ten Commandments (Ex. 20:12). Paul exhorted children to honor their parents, stating God's promised reward, "that it may be well with you and you may live long upon the earth" (Eph. 6:2-3). God established the family unit from the beginning, and there is a divine authority that works through it.

The fourth line of authority is to the individual. Every human being has a free will and each is independently responsible before God for his or her own actions. People have authority and responsibility for their own lives.

It is important that we recognize all four of these lines of authority and understand that each comes from God. We must respect these. People cause chaos and get into trouble when they cross the God-ordained authority lines. For example, the government is violating God-ordained authority when it tries to control the Church. Conversely, we have seen throughout history that the Church has gotten into trouble when she has tried to control the established government.

I am not teaching isolationism nor non-involvement. On the contrary, we must make an influence across authority lines. The Church is to shine the light, be the salt of the earth, and do all in her power to *influence* the government to follow godly paths. Similarly, each individual should attempt to influence their family in a positive fashion.

It is the "usurping of authority" against which I am teaching. Every established authority is established by God and, therefore, must be left accountable to God. That authority must not be violated.

This means that the Church has a certain line of authority, but she must not violate the authority God has established within the family or for the individual. She should teach, and Church leaders even may rebuke harshly at times, but she must not dictate what the families or individuals have to do in violation of their free wills.

Similarly, the family must allow each individual member to make decisions for his or her own personal life. Each individual must respect the established structure of the family. No one person should be allowed to control the Church or violate the government's authority. Each line of authority must be respected and recognized as accountable to God.

When people cross their line of authority, then they are no longer backed by God's authority nor His power. For example, if the family dictates to a member what he or she is to do, in violation of the individual's free will, then they are controlling and dominating in an evil manner. Similarly, if a church leader starts demanding that families or individuals do things, which should be decided only by themselves, then authority is being abused and God is not behind it. Evil forces (which we will explain as we continue) begin where God's authority ends.

Now the question of disobedience to authority arises. For example, should a Christian go against the dictates of the established government? When should an individual go against his spiritual leaders? I hesitate to answer the question, lest people take my understanding as an absolute rule to be applied mechanically. As each person is responsible before

God, each must decide for his own life. Similarly, the Church is responsible before God, therefore, she must determine God's will in each situation that is faced. Please understand this…we are talking about principles here, not legalistic dictates.

There are times when civil disobedience is appropriate, for we see in the book of Acts that the early disciples preached the Gospel even though the governmental authorities forbade them to do so (Acts 4:15-20). Note that the disciples were not exerting their authority over the local authorities. Rather, they were claiming the authority, which God already had given to them. This was not a case of the disciples crossing into the government's authority, but rather, the governmental officials crossing into the Church's authority and telling her not to speak what God had commissioned her to declare. The disciples were not violating authority, but they were claiming the authority, which was rightfully theirs.

This principle of claiming one's God-given authority holds true in the individual's life, as well. Every individual must have responsibility for his own life. If the family or the Church begins to dictate what the individual should do, in violation of individual freedom, then that person has a right to disobey. He is not being disobedient to God in exercising that right, because the family or Church, in such cases, has no authority from God to be domineering or controlling.

In all such circumstances, it is God-given authority that we must recognize. There is not just one line of authority, but four.

This is important because some leaders have been guilty of abusing authority and dominating people. Others have gone to the opposite extreme and made themselves timid because they were afraid of becoming overbearing. Both of these problems can be overcome simply by recognizing and respecting the four lines of authority God has established.

Those who are abusive need to realize that their authority ends where another's begins. Most cases of evil control and manipulation do not occur because a leader was too forceful or strong. Rather, they are the results of someone exercising authority outside of that which God has given.

At the other extreme are those who hold back from speaking and saying things because they are afraid of controlling others wrongfully. They, too, will find freedom only by hearing the truth. Freedom from evil control and manipulation does not come by making oneself wishy-washy. On the contrary, a person can be very bold and even forceful without releasing evil forces. There are many things over which leaders should take control. The key is that they stay within the authority God has given them. When a person knows he is in a God-given role, then he is not weak, but rather confident.

Leaders must know this. Only if they decide when and where God has given them authority will they fulfill God's purposes for their lives.[17]

The stories of Moses and David are not about the line of church authority; they are about the line of governmental authority. When leaders take these stories and pull them into the church context, they are crossing authority lines and abuse is inevitable.

In the Shepherding Movement of the 1970s, Watchman Nee's book, *Spiritual Authority*, clearly made this mistake and crossed these lines.[18] This book was foundational to the Shepherding Movement

[17] Eberle, Harold. *God's Leaders for Tomorrow's World*, (Yakima, WA: Worldcast Publishing, 2003) 7-12.

[18] Watchman Nee, *Spiritual Authority*, (New York, NY: Christian Fellowship Publishers, 1972).

and was the root theological cause of much of the resultant abuse. Following in Nee's footsteps, many other book titles were released in the early 2000s that spoke of "submission" and being "under covering." Unfortunately, these perpetuated the same mistake as Nee by applying the governmental authority line to the church authority line.

I don't believe that Nee[19] had any idea how toxic and destructive it is to cross authority lines. And sadly, the books that have been released from this point of view have left a path of control and abuse in their wake.

Many other leaders have written books—or will write books in the future—that make this mistake. The issue of authority and control is perennial. The bottom line for a fivefold leader is that we must move in a spirit that is the opposite of controlling others. We must move in *self-control* and teach others to move in self-control as well. When we control others, we are violating the fruit of the Spirit by removing another person's ability to be self-controlled.

RESIDUE WORDS

Residual terminology from the Shepherding Movement can act as a warning sign of control and hierarchy. Here, we will look at some of the red-flag words to watch out for. Not everyone means the same thing when using these terms, but I have observed misuse of the following:

[19] Watchman Nee has written many other books that I consider a blessing to the body of Christ. I do not include his name to be disrespectful. Please note that I am only taking issue with one small portion of his written teachings. The reason it is worth mentioning specifically is because this book has had massive impact within the Charismatic/Pentecostal movement. I appreciate and value Brother Nee and the body of work he has contributed.

Covering

The question, "Who is your covering?" is asked between Christians around the world on a daily basis. When people ask this, essentially they mean: Who is above you? Who is the authority over your spiritual walk? Who is your denominational leader or local pastor?

The idea of covering is based on the idea that all Christians are a part of a cosmic hierarchy and that by submitting to the spiritual person above us, we will be spiritually protected and God will be more pleased with us. The reality is, the word *covering* appears only once in the New Testament and refers to first-century female head coverings:

> *…but that if a woman has long hair, it is her glory? For long hair is given to her as a covering.* (1 Cor. 11:15)

Though many leaders like to talk about the idea of covering as though it's biblical, such an idea is a fantasy. The Bible gives us no concept of "spiritual covering."

> *Now **it is God who makes both us and you stand firm in Christ.** He anointed us, set his seal of ownership on us, and put his Spirit in our hearts as a deposit, guaranteeing what is to come. I call God as my witness—and I stake my life on it—that it was in order to spare you that I did not return to Corinth. **Not that we lord it over your faith, but we work with you for your joy, because it is by faith you stand firm.** (2 Cor. 1:21-24)*

In the body of Christ, people are not over other people. Yet some do have the fivefold calling, and that means they carry a grace to serve. Apostles carry more grace to serve than prophets, and prophets more than teachers, and so on.

Subjection

Second, the word *subjection* is commonly used to describe our duty toward positional authority. The New Testament does teach us to be subject to certain human authority structures:

1. ***Children are subject to their parents:***

   Children, obey your parents in the Lord, for this is right. (Eph. 6:1)

   Children, obey your parents in everything, for this pleases the Lord. (Col. 3:20)

2. ***Employees are subject to their employers:***

   Slaves, obey your earthly masters with respect and fear, and with sincerity of heart, just as you would obey Christ. (Eph. 6:5)

   Slaves, obey your earthly masters in everything; and do it, not only when their eye is on you and to curry their favor, but with sincerity of heart and reverence for the Lord. (Col. 3:22)

3. ***Citizens are subject to their government rulers:***

   Remind the people to be subject to rulers and authorities, to be obedient, to be ready to do whatever is good. (Titus 3:1)

However, subjection does not mean one-hundred-percent obedience. Subjection is an attitude of the heart, which aims to honor and respect the position of the leader, even when obedience is inappropriate. For example, it would have been evil for the Hebrew midwives to obey Pharaoh by killing Hebrew babies (see Exod. 1:17), for Daniel to stop praying (see Dan. 6:8– 10), or for the apostles to stop preaching Christ (see Acts 4:18–20; 5:27–29):

The midwives, however, feared God and did not do what the king of Egypt had told them to do; they let the boys live. (Ex. 1:17)

Now, Your Majesty, issue the decree and put it in writing so that it cannot be altered—in accordance with the law of the Medes and Persians, which cannot be repealed." So King Darius put the decree in writing.

Now when Daniel learned that the decree had been published, he went home to his upstairs room where the windows opened toward Jerusalem. Three times a day he got down on his knees and prayed, giving thanks to his God, just as he had done before. (Dan. 6:8-10)

Then they called them in again and commanded them not to speak or teach at all in the name of Jesus. But Peter and John replied, "Which is right in God's eyes: to listen to you, or to him? You be the judges! As for us, we cannot help speaking about what we have seen and heard." (Acts 4:18-20)

The apostles were brought in and made to appear before the Sanhedrin to be questioned by the high priest. "We gave you strict orders not to teach in this name," he said. "Yet you have filled Jerusalem with your teaching and are determined to make us guilty of this man's blood."

Peter and the other apostles replied: "We must obey God rather than human beings!" (Acts 5:27-29)

EQUIPPING THE EQUIPPERS

Obedience is not always right, but we are to be subject to certain positional authority structures in society. Being subject to those authorities means that we treat their position with the respect that it carries, not that we always obey.

Obedience

Third is the word *obedience*, which is closely related to the idea of subjection. The Bible makes it clear we are to be obedient to Christ:

> *Jesus replied, "Anyone who loves me will obey my teaching. My Father will love them, and we will come to them and make our home with them. Anyone who does not love me will not obey my teaching. These words you hear are not my own; they belong to the Father who sent me." (*John 14:23-24)

> *"Remember what I told you: 'A servant is not greater than his master.' If they persecuted me, they will persecute you also. If they obeyed my teaching, they will obey yours also." (*John 15:20)

The debate is over whether or not we must obey church leadership. While *must* implies compulsory obedience, the New Testament teaches us to voluntarily yield to the experience and Christlikeness of godly leaders in our lives. (This is another way of saying "submit yourselves to.") Yet those who believe in compulsory obedience point to one passage in particular that seems to support authoritarianism:

> *Remember them which have the **rule over you**, who have spoken unto you the word of God: whose faith follow, considering the end of their conversation . . . (*Hebrews 13:7 KJV)

124

> ***Obey them that have the rule over you***, *and submit yourselves: for they watch for your souls, as they that must give account, that they may do it with joy, and not with grief: for that is unprofitable for you.* (Hebrews 13:17 KJV)

The King James Version of these passages contain several harsh mistranslations, as highlighted above. Thankfully, the NIV has translated these verses in a more accurate and appropriate manner:

> *Remember your leaders, who spoke the word of God to you. Consider the outcome of their way of life and imitate their faith. . . . . Have confidence in your leaders and submit to their authority, because they keep watch over you as those who must give an account. Do this so that their work will be a joy, not a burden, for that would be of no benefit to you.* (Heb. 13:7, 17)

Here we see that the command is not unequivocal obedience but respect for and imitation of leaders who have influenced us positively. Also "submit to their authority" is not about position. Authority equals foot-washing, therefore, submitting means letting them serve you. Peter had to let Jesus wash his feet and thereby submitted to Jesus, "authority."

Submission

Fourth, we have the idea of *submission*. Many have interpreted this term in a hierarchical sense, but the new covenant concept of leadership is not built on a hierarchy containing levels of submission. All are equal in the body of Christ, and all submit to all. Submission is required by all to all. Submission is mutual and changes moment by moment. Sometimes I submit to my pastor; sometimes he submits to me. Sometimes I submit to my wife; at other times she submits to me. In the new covenant, *submission is never a one-way street*. Here is how the apostles Paul and Peter put it:

Submit to one another out of reverence for Christ. (Eph. 5:21)

In the same way, you who are younger, submit yourselves to your elders. All of you, clothe yourselves with humility toward one another . . . (1 Peter 5:5a)

These passages are admonishments. Paul and Peter are appealing to their listeners to submit to each other. They are not demanding, ordering, or commanding like a controlling leader might. A true new covenant leader respects the fact that we all belong to Christ and none of us should control another. Each one is to be self-controlled, not controlled by others. Therefore, it is not right for a leader to push, coerce, or force others' decisions. Instead, we are to appeal to the hearts of those we lead. We see an incredible display of this in Paul's letter to Philemon:

*Therefore, although in Christ I could be bold and order you to do what you ought to do, **yet I prefer to appeal to you on the basis of love.** It is as none other than Paul—an old man and now also a prisoner of Christ Jesus—**that I appeal to you** for my son Onesimus, who became my son while I was in chains.*

Formerly he was useless to you, but now he has become useful both to you and to me.

*I am sending him—who is my very heart—back to you. **I would have liked to keep him** with me so that he could take your place in helping me while I am in chains for the gospel. **But I did not want to do anything without your consent,** so that any favor you do **would not seem forced but would be voluntary** . . . I,*

Paul, am writing this with my own hand. I will pay it back—
not to mention that you owe me your very self. (Philem. 1:8-14,
19)

Here Paul says he could be more demanding, on the basis that he was
the one who had preached the gospel to Philemon (*"not to mention*
that you owe me your very self "), yet he chose not to take that route.
Instead, Paul appealed to him on the basis of their relationship and
all that Paul had done to earn the right to ask this of Philemon.

At other times, Paul modeled this same approach when he sent
out a fellow worker with his personal approval, asking those who
received that worker to treat him or her with a due level of respect:

When Timothy comes, see to it that he has nothing to fear while
he is with you, for he is carrying on the work of the Lord, just as
I am. No one, then, should treat him with contempt. Send him
on his way in peace so that he may return to me. I am expecting
him along with the brothers . . . You know that the household
of Stephanas were the first converts in Achaia, and they have
devoted themselves to the service of the Lord's people. I urge you,
brothers and sisters, to submit to such people and to everyone who
joins in the work and labors at it. I was glad when Stephanas,
Fortunatus and Achaicus arrived, because they have supplied what
was lacking from you. For they refreshed my spirit and yours also.
Such men deserve recognition. (1 Cor. 16:10-11, 15-18)

I am sending him to you for this very purpose, that you may know
how we are, and that he may encourage you. (Eph. 6:22)

Paul was essentially saying that these individuals were *worthy* people
to submit to. He was not saying, "You must submit to them. They are

higher than you, and I have ordained them. Therefore, you must obey them unconditionally."

Clearly, submission is mutual and voluntary, and it is given to those who have earned it through relationship, not simply because of position.

What are we submitting to? We are submitting to those who will sacrifice on our behalf like Christ (Eph. 5), or who will be kneeling in front of us to wash our feet (John 13). We do not submit to positions in the body of Christ, because there is no positional authority. We submit to the grace someone has on their life, especially if we are in their sphere to serve us.

Governing

"Governing" typically comes from interpreting the kingdom of God as the government of God. Therefore, fivefold ministers must be the officers of His government, called to rule over the "sheeple." This creates a hierarchy, which is not based on the great leader being the greater servant, and Matthew 20:25-28 is instantly violated:

> *Jesus called them together and said, "You know that the rulers of the Gentiles lord it over them, and their high officials exercise authority over them. Not so with you. Instead, whoever wants to become great among you must be your servant, and whoever wants to be first must be your slave—just as the Son of Man did not come to be served, but to serve, and to give his life as a ransom for many." (Matt. 20:25-28)*

Yet the leader cannot see this because of their leanings toward an overemphasis on God's sovereignty, and the idea that we should all be controlling like God is controlling. This belief spills over into everybody in the body having "covenant relationships" that overrule the individual's ability to be self-controlled and to personally discern the Spirit's will.

Wise leaders can offer direction and correction, but they should not be controlling. Instead, they take responsibility for their actions and help those they lead to do the same.

A FEW MORE THOUGHTS

We are all given authority over the demonic realm (Luke 10:18-20), and we have all been given access to God (Heb. 4:16), and have been made priests (Rev 5:10):

> *He replied, "I saw Satan fall like lightning from heaven. I have given you authority to trample on snakes and scorpions and to overcome all the power of the enemy; nothing will harm you. However, do not rejoice that the spirits submit to you, but rejoice that your names are written in heaven."* (Luke 10:18-20)

> *Let us then approach God's throne of grace with confidence, so that we may receive mercy and find grace to help us in our time of need.* (Heb. 4:16)

> *You have made them to be a kingdom and priests to serve our God, and they will reign on the earth* (Rev. 5:10)

We are all *priests unto God*: We all have direct access and nobody should get in the way of that access. But not all of us are *priests to the body of Christ*: Some have been put in as "overseers" or "elders," which are made up of those with the grace and metron of being fivefold leaders:

Keep watch over yourselves and all the flock of which the Holy Spirit has made you overseers. Be shepherds of the church of God, which he bought with his own blood. (Acts 20:28)

Paul and Timothy, servants of Christ Jesus, To all God's holy people in Christ Jesus at Philippi, together with the overseers and deacons . . . (Phil. 1:1)

The reason I left you in Crete was that you might put in order what was left unfinished and appoint elders in every town, as I directed you. (Titus 1:5)

To the elders among you, I appeal as a fellow elder and a witness of Christ's sufferings who also will share in the glory to be revealed . . . (1 Peter 5:1)

Is anyone among you sick? Let them call the elders of the church to pray over them and anoint them with oil in the name of the Lord . . . (James 5:14)

The elders who direct the affairs of the church well are worthy of double honor, especially those whose work is preaching and teaching . . . (1 Tim. 5:17)

Paul and Barnabas appointed elders for them in each church and, with prayer and fasting, committed them to the Lord, in whom they had put their trust . . . (Acts 14:23)

We don't want to flatten the body of Christ and swing too far in the other direction into being those who "reject authority" (Jude 8) or "despise authority" (2 Peter 2:10).

There are greater and lesser authorities, defined entirely by the measure of servanthood—your metron, in which God graced you to serve.

We have seen plenty of things to guard against. What do we want to embrace?

Honor

Lastly, we have a positive term, *honor*. When we give honor to people, we create an invisible platform under their feet. We give them more of a right to speak into our lives and increased ease to do so.

I have experienced this many times in churches where I have traveled to speak. If the local pastor stands before the people and tells them about me, the impact I have had on his or her life, and how excited, grateful, and honored they are to have me there, those who have come to hear me teach will get a lot more out of the time. This is because the pastor has created an invisible platform in the atmosphere that I can step out on, enabling me to get the meeting going very easily. I have also experienced churches where the pastor doesn't understand these dynamics and simply stands before the people and says, "Let's welcome our guest speaker, Jonathan Welton!" In these cases, the people attending have no idea how to receive me or what my host feels about me. It is very awkward and makes my job much harder.

Honor works this way in every setting. Imagine a friend introduces me by saying, "This is my friend, Dr. Jonathan Welton. I have known him for twenty years, he's one of my closest friends, and he is an author, theologian, and respected apostle." By saying this, my friend has laid a foundation of honor that will impact how I am received. Compare that to someone simply saying, "This is my friend, Jonathan."

Once we recognize these dynamics, it is important to carefully decide to whom we will give an invisible platform in our lives. Simply put: what we honor, we create room for, and what we honor, we imitate. That is why Paul urged his readers, on multiple occasions, to imitate him:

> *I am writing this not to shame you but to warn you as my dear children. Even if you had ten thousand guardians in Christ, you do not have many fathers, for in Christ Jesus I became your father through the gospel. Therefore I urge you to imitate me. For this reason I have sent to you Timothy, my son whom I love, who is faithful in the Lord. He will remind you of my way of life in Christ Jesus, which agrees with what I teach everywhere in every church.* (1 Cor. 4:14-17).

> *Follow my example, as I follow the example of Christ.* (1 Cor. 11:1).

> *Join together in following my example, brothers and sisters, and just as you have us as a model, keep your eyes on those who live as we do.* (Phil. 3:17)

> *Whatever you have learned or received or heard from me, or seen in me—put it into practice. And the God of peace will be with you.* (Phil. 4:9)

> *You became imitators of us and of the Lord, for you welcomed the message in the midst of severe suffering with the joy given by the Holy Spirit.* (1 Thess. 1:6)

In other words, Paul was encouraging his readers— those who honored him—to also imitate him. He was saying, "Don't simply put me on a pedestal; truly honor me by imitating me, as I honor Christ by imitating Him."

Imitation does not mean we lose our uniqueness. It does not mean we become a copy. It means that we see Christ flowing through people in unique ways, and we receive from them. As new creations in Christ, our identity is secure in Him. We do not find our identity in connection with or imitation of certain leaders—that is not what I am talking about. However, opening our hearts to receive from and be influenced by our mentors, including those we may never meet, is an important part of Christian honor. When we honor leaders in this way, we accelerate our own growth and our ability to lead and influence others positively.

FINAL THOUGHTS

From this brief look at the inflammatory words often used in the context of leadership, we have seen that the Bible's standard for leadership is not at all about control or required obedience. Instead, biblical leaders lay down their lives for those they serve, just as Jesus laid down His life for us. We see this so clearly in Peter's admonition to leaders:

> *Be shepherds of God's flock that is under your care, watching over them—not because you must, but because you are willing, as God wants you to be; not pursuing dishonest gain, but eager to serve; not lording it over those entrusted to you, but being examples to the flock.* (1 Peter 5:2–3)

Leadership is not an obligation or an opportunity for power. Instead, it is the privilege to serve others wholeheartedly and honestly. May we embrace that privilege with hearts of love for the people we serve.

CHAPTER EIGHT

BRINGING CORRECTION

We have examined how leaders have a sphere of influence and how those spheres can differ in size based on the grace on a leader's life. Before moving on, I must mention some very unpopular but important things.

Fivefold leaders must bring correction within their sphere of influence. We see this all throughout the New Testament. Jesus Himself had to correct those in His own sphere of influence many times:

To Peter: *"Get behind me Satan."* (Matt. 16:23)

To James and John: *"You do not know what spirit you are of."* (Luke 9:55)

To Judas: *"You will always have the poor with you."* (John 12:8)

To Peter: *"If you don't let me wash your feet, you have no part with me."* (John 13:8)

Dealing with difficult people issues as a fivefold leader can bring great discouragement and even despair. Jesus Himself declared, *"How long must I put up with you!"* (Matt. 17:17; Mark 9:19; Luke

9:41). Paul, speaking of the challenges his ministry faced, wrote, *"We despaired of life itself"* (2 Cor. 1:8-9). Paul also wrote, *"I was appointed as an apostle and teacher, that is why I am suffering as I am"* (2 Tim. 1:11-12).

Trying to adjust the spiritual bones of God's people ("to equip" them, Eph. 4:12) can be incredibly tiresome and involve a lot of rejection, but God has poured out His grace on true fivefold leaders to make these adjustments in the body. Many Christian leaders have quickly fallen out of ministry because they were not graced for the ministry task they took on.

Yes, bringing correction is difficult. Yes, it is the most thankless part of our job. But it is required of fivefold leaders because we are the only ones with the grace to do it.

Today, it is often considered disrespectful to "name names," meaning that if you disagree with a concept, you teach against the concept, but you do not point out who is teaching it. Yet in the New Testament, we see confrontation handled very directly. I believe that this is the difference between when a pastor-grace confronts issues versus when an apostle-grace confronts issues. Apostles are very strong and direct, and because the church has become used to more gentle pastors, they have lost touch with what an apostle feels like. Therefore, when apostles arise to confront specific theology or individuals, their confidence level can seem arrogant and their correction can shock people.

Let's closely examine how the New Testament apostles confronted theology, sin, and specific people. This is a long list, but its length proves the need for the confrontation I'm describing:

Paul declared to Elymas the Sorcerer, *"You son of the devil, you enemy of all righteousness, full of all deceit and villainy, will you not stop making crooked the straight paths of the Lord?"* (Acts 13:10).

Paul rebuked the Corinthian man for sleeping with his stepmother (1 Cor. 5:1-5).

Paul was so forceful he even rebuked Peter to his face (Gal. 2:11-16).

To the Judaizers, who taught circumcision, Paul declares his wish that they would just emasculate themselves (Gal. 5:10-12)!

Paul tells the Philippians to *"Watch out for those dogs, those evildoers, those mutilators of the flesh,"* in reference to the Judaizers (Phil. 3:2).

Paul, speaking again of the Judaizers, says that they are *"puffed up by idle notions in their unspiritual mind"* (Col. 2:16-19).

When someone claimed to have instruction from Paul about the "Lord's day" having already come, Paul corrects this falsehood (2 Thess. 2:1-3).

Alexander, Hymenaeus, and Philetus are condemned for their blasphemous teaching, which spread like gangrene (1 Tim. 1:20; 2 Tim. 2:17-18).

Paul says to insist on certain teachings, and if someone disagrees, then *"they are conceited and understand nothing"* (1 Tim. 6:4).

Again regarding the Judaizers, Paul says they have a form of godliness but deny its power; their folly will become clear to everyone (2 Tim. 3:5-9).

Paul was very direct about a local idol maker: *"Alexander the coppersmith did me great harm; the Lord will repay him according to his deeds. Beware of him yourself, for he strongly opposed our message"* (2 Tim. 4:14-15).

"For there are many rebellious people, full of meaningless talk and deception, especially those of the circumcision group. They must be silenced, because they are disrupting whole households by teaching things they ought not to teach—and that for the sake of dishonest gain. One of Crete's own prophets has said it: 'Cretans are always liars, evil brutes, lazy gluttons.' This saying is true. Therefore rebuke them sharply, so that they will be sound in the faith and will pay no attention to Jewish myths or to the merely human commands of those who reject the truth." (Titus 1:10-14)

Warn a divisive person once, and then warn them a second time. After that, have nothing to do with them (Titus 3:10).

We find in 2 Peter 2-3:5 a parallel to the entire book of Jude. Both passages describe a group of false teachers who were present in the early church. Peter and Jude go to great lengths describing and condemning them.

When John writes his letters and confronts the Gnostic heretics, he refers to them as "antichrist" (1 John 2:18, 20-22, 4:2-3; 2 John 7).

And in 3 John 9-10, he names Diotrephes, who apparently was a very controlling individual.

In Revelation 2-3, Jesus confronts many groups. He calls one Jezebel, some are Nicolaitans, some are a synagogue of Satan, and some are like Balaam.

In almost every letter written after the Gospels, there are specific theological warnings and corrections of false teachers. Paul even warned the Ephesian elders that savage wolves would come from their own congregation to attack the church (Acts 20:28-31).

THE BOTTOM LINE

When a fivefold leader brings correction, other fivefold leaders typically appreciate it. True, fivefold-graced leaders are okay with being confronted because they understand that they are held to a higher and public standard (James 3:1, 1 Tim. 3, Titus 1). It is the non-fivefold members of the body who typically get angry because they like the false teaching. And though there are many reasons why the typical Christian may get upset, correction is often near the top of the list, because it is seen as "mean."

Correction will be painful at times, but the only way to deal with gangrene (2 Tim. 2:17) is to amputate; it might hurt in the short term, but it will allow the body to survive in the long term. We cannot allow people to have their ears tickled (2 Tim. 4:3) by false teachings; we must boldly confront the teachings and those who teach them.

As ever, we would be wise to follow the example of Jesus and the apostles:

Jesus called certain people children of the devil (John 8:44), children of hell (Matt. 23:15), blind fools (Matt. 23:17), snakes (Matt. 23:33), empty tombs (Matt. 23:27), Jezebel, Balaam, and a synagogue of Satan.

Paul referred to some as gangrene, dogs, mutilators of the flesh, savage wolves, unspiritual, and understanding nothing. And he wished some would just emasculate themselves.

Peter and Jude said that some were clouds without rain, some were blots and blemishes, and some are like Balaam and return to their own vomit.

John called some people antichrists.

This is heavy stuff. But it's vital. We have come a long way from the New Testament model of boldly confronting. Nowadays, if you suggest that a teaching is false, silly, or stupid, the offense level from other Christians is astounding. Yet people would be less shocked if they actually were familiar with the ways of the New Testament leaders. In comparison, modern confrontation is quite gentle.

If I may, I want to give you the same charge that Paul gave Timothy:

> *In the presence of God and of Christ Jesus, who will judge the living and the dead, and in view of his appearing and his kingdom, I give you this charge: Preach the word; be prepared in season and out of season; correct, rebuke and encourage—with great patience and careful instruction. For the time will come when people will not put up with sound doctrine. Instead, to suit their own desires, they will gather around them a great number of teachers to say what their itching ears want to hear. They will turn their ears away from the truth and turn aside to myths. But you, keep your head in all situations, endure hardship, do the work of an evangelist, discharge all the duties of your ministry.* (2 Tim. 4:1-5)

CHAPTER NINE

TRUE FIVEFOLD LEADERS

I am writing this not to shame you but to warn you as my dear children. Even if you had ten thousand guardians in Christ, you do not have many fathers, for in Christ Jesus I became your father through the gospel. Therefore I urge you to imitate me. (1 Cor. 4:14-16)

True fivefold leaders are fathers. Fathers don't control; they offer wisdom, advice, and guidance. The goal of a father is to raise a mature child who is completely self-controlled. *The fruit of the Spirit is not submission; the fruit of the spirit is self-control.* The goal is not to have someone under you; the goal is for you to raise them to be equals.

Paul focused more on people imitating him than he did on people submitting to him. Submitting to God is the major point in the New Testament, but submitting to church leaders is a lesser focus.

Fathers set an example, and we want to follow their example. Fathers aren't our personal accountability partners. They may not come to your house and do a personal Bible study with you. I say this because many people place unrealistic expectations on their spiritual fathers. It is not that they will constantly be at your side, pushing you forward. Unless you have a close personal relationship like Paul did with Timothy, that is not going to happen. Yet Paul wrote to the whole church in Corinth and addressed them as their spiritual father. Surely not all of them had a close relationship with Paul, and yet he was still their father. What we should see in a spiritual father is that they are "fatherly." They lovingly speak the wisdom and guidance we need, and they can also humbly receive correction themselves.

Paul was not only fatherly; he even refers to his care for the Thessalonians in motherly, nurturing terms:

> *Instead, we were like young children among you. Just as a nursing mother cares for her children, so we cared for you. Because we loved you so much, we were delighted to share with you not only the gospel of God but our lives as well.* (1 Thess. 2:7-8)

SPIRITUAL FATHERS

While much could be written about "spiritual fathers," I want to simply outline seven positive functions and seven pitfalls to avoid in this area. Let's begin with the positive side of spiritual fathers:

1. They provide. Jesus did not have interns. He didn't charge His apostles to travel with Him. When He said, "Come follow me," the implication was that they would follow and He would provide. He was a good provider too; He even had a treasurer (John 13:29). (More on this in the pitfalls section below.)

2. They protect. Paul protected the church at Antioch from Peter's hypocrisy by confronting him publicly and directly (Gal. 2:11). Also Paul informs the Ephesians that when he leaves them, spiritual "wolves" will attack them. Yet when Paul was present, they were protected (Acts 20:29-31).

3. They correct. I have addressed this point at length in the chapter on correction, but it is important that it is included on this list.[20]

4. They speak love and value. Paul's spiritual children never had to wonder how he felt about them. He was intensely expressive as a spiritual father, constantly encouraging them to greet one another with a kiss, to treat one another like family, to be kind, gentle, and supportive of one another. He also shared passionately about his longing to be together with them, saying that he felt orphaned when he wasn't with them (1 Thess. 2:17).

5. They promote you. Good spiritual fathers are focused on the future and passing the work of leadership to the next generation. They will actively stand behind and promote their sons. We see Jesus doing this by pouring into His disciples, and Paul stands behind Timothy and Titus in many of his letters. It is especially clear in this passage: *"I hope in the Lord Jesus to send Timothy to you soon, that I also may be cheered when I receive news about you. I have no one else like him, who will show genuine concern for your welfare. For everyone looks out for their own interests, not those of Jesus Christ. But you know that Timothy has proved himself, because as a son with his father he has served with me in the work of the gospel"* (Phil. 2:19-22).

6. They pray for you. We know that Jesus prayed for His disciples in John 17:6-19, and also He prayed specifically for Peter to make it through Satan's sifting (Luke 22:31). I appreciate the way that Paul wrote out many of his prayers in his letters, but specifically how he embraced the labor of prayer over his spiritual sons: *"My dear*

---

[20] As my friend, Allison Armerding, has suggested, "Perhaps the modern church is soft on and easily offended by correction because we aren't a family? If we had fiercer love and commitment to one another, we would more bravely and directly confront one another, for we would recognize that in doing so, we are loving one another and fighting for our maturity and connection. In Hebrews 12, we see that the Father corrects and disciplines us as sons and daughters because He loves us. The more the Father's heart is restored to the church, the more we will appreciate correction and build a healthy culture of correction."

children, for whom I am again in the pains of childbirth until Christ is formed in you" (Gal. 4:19).

7. They focus their attention on you. Jesus had crowds that followed Him, and seventy disciples that He empowered, but He only had twelve apostles and He specifically washed their feet. Also, when He prayed, He said, *"I have revealed you to those whom you gave me out of the world. They were yours; you gave them to me and they have obeyed your word"* (John 17:6). This shows that Jesus knew whom the Father had given Him. We must also know whom the Father has given us. Paul also knew who was in his metron (1 Cor. 9:2, 2 Cor. 10:13).

SEVEN PITFALLS

Although many may use the term "spiritual father," there are some common mistakes and character issues that have tainted many against valuing true spiritual fathering. Here are the top seven that I have witnessed:

1. An accountability partner. A spiritual father is not an accountability partner always focusing on your sin and stumbling. Too often, when an individual grabs on to the idea of "spiritual fathering," it very quickly becomes a weekly meeting at a café where the previous week's struggles are rehashed. I can't imagine Jesus or the apostle Paul doing this, yet it seems to be the "go-to" idea for modern spiritual fathering. Yet the reality is that a good father in the natural wouldn't even focus on a child's struggles and mistakes. Instead, a good father would encourage their passions and dreams and push them to move forward confidently.

2. Violation of self-control. I have already said much in this book regarding self-control, yet it bears repeating. A good spiritual father is like Jesus, and Jesus never violated His followers' self-control. To grow a child into a fully matured son is to teach them how to have personal ownership and responsibility for their own life and choices.

3. Elijah replaces Jesus. Many teachings on spiritual fathering try to use Elijah as the model. I believe this creates room for a lot of error. Elijah's personality had some problems. For example, look at the level of insecurity he displayed when Jezebel threatened him (1 Kings 19:3-4). Then when the disciples of Jesus tried to act like Elijah and call fire down on Samaria, Jesus rebuked them for it! (Luke 9:55) I suggest that we follow Jesus as our model of what a spiritual father looks like.

4. Everyone must be fathered. The idea that you "cannot father because you haven't been fathered" gets a lot of circulation, but doesn't hold up under examination. Yes, Joshua had Moses, Elisha had Elijah, and Timothy had Paul, but who was Moses' spiritual father? Who was Elijah's spiritual father? Who was Paul's spiritual father?[21] Who was Jesus' spiritual father? Where does the multi-level system of fathering end? You can "align yourself" under someone who is aligned under someone, who is aligned under someone, but eventually the chain will end with some individual who doesn't have someone over them. Is it okay that they do not have a father over them? I say yes, because this multi-level system was never ordained anyway. A spiritual father is an incredible blessing, but if you don't have one, it shouldn't leave you feeling like an orphan. We need to stand on our own two feet spiritually and have our secure identity come from Father God first. Then a spiritual father can be a blessing to us and pour into us and we will receive it, rather than leaking out the blessing through insecurity.

5. They are a financial burden. Rather than spiritual fathers providing finances to their sons to advance the kingdom, the modern system of "apostolic networks" is so broken that spiritual fathers demand that spiritual sons provide for them! The apostle Paul said

[21] Although we have nothing that points to Paul's spiritual father, we do have mention of who might perhaps be considered Paul's "spiritual mom" in Romans 16:13: "Greet Rufus, chosen in the Lord, and his mother, who has been a mother to me, too."

it well when he wrote: *"I will not be a burden to you, because what I want is not your possessions but you. After all, children should not have to save up for their parents, but parents for their children. So I will very gladly spend for you everything I have and expend myself as well"* (2 Cor. 12:14-15).

6. They take value from you. Rather than standing behind you and promoting you, many "spiritual fathers" have "adopted" sons that make them look good. It is exciting to link yourself to a young person who is seeing thousands saved on the mission field. It makes fathers look good. Yet when the same son makes a mistake, the father isn't there to help him back on to his feet. This is a self-serving version of fathering.

7. They are not approachable. Many "spiritual fathers" are cold and distant. They believe that sons should pursue them and they do not set the example in pursuing. Yet Father God pursued all of humanity to the point of sending His Son to reconcile the world to Himself. Jesus humbled Himself and became flesh to win us back from sin and death. Jesus washed the feet of His bride before His bride was required to respond (Eph. 5). The example Jesus gives in the story of the prodigal son is one of a father who pursues. No, he didn't follow the younger son out into the brothels, but when the son returns, the older brother leaves the party and the father pursues him. In that ancient culture, the elder son leaving the party was an insult that would have gotten him stoned to death. The father instead chooses to go out and pursue him and plead with him to come back in.

Fathers are meant to be soft and approachable. We know even God Himself as "Abba," as Daddy-God. Spiritual fathers are meant to be papas, daddies, and kind, approachable leaders. Yes, they should be strong, but we shouldn't be afraid of being openhearted with them.

AGE

Lastly, one of the issues that is often brought up about spiritual fathering is the issue of age.

In Isaiah 9:6, Jesus is referred to as the *"Everlasting Father."* Even though we may or may not have a spiritual father while we are going through life, we all have a spiritual father in Jesus Himself.

This also speaks to the awkwardness that some have regarding a spiritual father who is younger than they are. Yet Jesus has spiritually fathered us all, while being 30-33 years old. The disciples were quite young, and the learned rabbis had to humble themselves when they came into the kingdom to learn from these young men. Timothy, the protégé of Paul, was also quite young, and yet Paul tells him not to get tripped up by his age (1 Tim. 4:12).

Having a spiritual father simply means that they are ahead of you in spiritual maturity, not that they are physically older. Many seventy-year-olds need to be humble enough to learn from thirty-year-olds, as much as the younger should learn from the elder's decades of life experience.

TRUE APOSTLES ARE ARCHITECTS

By the grace God has given me, I laid a foundation as a wise builder, and someone else is building on it. But each one should build with care. (1 Cor. 3:10)

Apostles, like architects, provide the blueprints, and then people with their own self-control can choose to follow them. Yet if we stray from the blueprints, the fivefold will "equip us" (which, if you remember, means to set a bone like a chiropractor).

Sometimes architects are wrong or outdated by using old codes, and others will correct them. Of the fivefold ministries, the apostle is specifically identified with the architect. I believe this shows us that they are the general overseer of building the church. The other four of the fivefold will follow the guidance and direction of the apostle. The apostle will serve them by directing the work with humility and wisdom.

Fivefold ministers carry the following messages:

1. Gender Equality

> *There is neither Jew nor Gentile, neither slave nor free, nor is there male and female, for you are all one in Christ Jesus.* (Gal. 3:28)

Many fivefold leaders are still confused by the three passages in the New Testament that seem to say women shouldn't be in leadership. If you are not teaching and leading the way in equality between the genders, I recommend you read Appendix Two: "Women in Leadership." It will bring right alignment in this area of equality. True fivefold leaders should be leading the way in bringing equality and removing oppression. This is also true of race equality and age-discrimination. When Jesus tore down the walls between Jews and Gentiles, He tore down the walls between all races:

> *You, however, must teach what is appropriate to sound doctrine. Teach the older men to be temperate, worthy of respect, self-controlled, and sound in faith, in love and in endurance.*
>
> *Likewise, teach the older women to be reverent in the way they live, not to be slanderers or addicted to much wine, but to teach what is good. Then they can urge the younger women to love their husbands and children, to be self-controlled and pure, to be busy*

at home, to be kind, and to be subject to their husbands, so that no one will malign the word of God.

Similarly, encourage the young men to be self-controlled. In everything set them an example by doing what is good. In your teaching show integrity, seriousness and soundness of speech that cannot be condemned, so that those who oppose you may be ashamed because they have nothing bad to say about us. (Titus 2:1-8)

All races and ages should be running together in the kingdom. We all have our own strengths, *and* we all need each other's strengths.

2. Family Atmosphere

Do not rebuke an older man harshly, but exhort him as if he were your father. Treat younger men as brothers, older women as mothers, and younger women as sisters, with absolute purity. (1 Tim. 5:1-2)

In this passage, Paul gives every group a place in the church family. A true fivefold ministry will feel like family; everybody has a place of belonging.

3. Fully Supernatural

Very truly I tell you, whoever believes in me will do the works I have been doing, and they will do even greater things than these, because I am going to the Father. (John 14:12)

And these signs will accompany those who believe: In my name

> *they will drive out demons; they will speak in new tongues; they will pick up snakes with their hands; and when they drink deadly poison, it will not hurt them at all; they will place their hands on sick people, and they will get well."*
>
> *After the Lord Jesus had spoken to them, he was taken up into heaven and he sat at the right hand of God. Then the disciples went out and preached everywhere, and the Lord worked with them and confirmed his word by the signs that accompanied it.* (Mark 16:17-20)

> *God also testified to it by signs, wonders and various miracles, and by gifts of the Holy Spirit distributed according to his will.* (Heb. 2:4)

True fivefold ministry isn't just a form or a structure; it is like the wiring of the kingdom. When functioning properly, a current of power will be carried and released. Beware of those who claim to be fivefold yet are not moving in the supernatural (2 Cor. 12:12).

4. The Advancing Kingdom

> *He told them another parable: "The kingdom of heaven is like a mustard seed, which a man took and planted in his field. Though it is the smallest of all seeds, yet when it grows, it is the largest of garden plants and becomes a tree, so that the birds come and perch in its branches."*
>
> *He told them still another parable: "The kingdom of heaven is like yeast that a woman took and mixed into about sixty pounds of flour until it worked all through the dough."* (Matt. 13:31-33)

The fivefold ministry is focused on advancing the kingdom, not simply growing a church or a denomination. Fivefold leaders are able to see a much bigger goal and push people toward it.

5. Healthy Self-Control

> *You, my brothers and sisters, were called to be free. But do not use your freedom to indulge the flesh; rather, serve one another humbly in love . . .*
>
> *But the fruit of the Spirit is love, joy, peace, forbearance, kindness, goodness, faithfulness, gentleness and self-control.* (Gal. 5:13, 22-23)

True fivefold leaders do not create co-dependent or subservient relationships. They build strong, self-controlled individuals who walk in their own metron, using the grace on their life.

THE NECESSARY CONDITIONS FOR SUBMISSION

I have authority. I have people that have submitted to me. Because of bad experiences with controlling leaders, that sentence may be hard for some to hear. The people who have submitted to me, love being submitted to me. Again, this could be hard to hear. But I will share with you the principle that makes submission a positive word.

It is imperative that leaders stoop to wash the feet of their followers. The action of "submission" required on the part of the follower is to "allow" their feet to be washed.

Jesus stooped to wash Peter's feet in John 13, but Peter wasn't going to allow Jesus to do something so "beneath" His station. Peter didn't want a servant leader; he wanted a royal boss—someone large and in charge, the kind of leader who cuts off ears like he would.

To receive a foot-washing from our leader requires that we submit ourselves. We are not submitting to control, we are submitting to service.

In many circles, you can hear talk of wives submitting to their husbands—as if God is mainly concerned with patriarchal structure. The submission verses in Ephesians 5 are typically the ones used to push submission on women. The often-overlooked piece of the puzzle is that the wife is to submit as the church submits to Christ. Christ is the One who "laid down His life for His bride." We have too quickly read over that part and over-emphasized the submission part.

In Ephesians 5, we also find the foot-washing principle. Christ first had to live, die, and rise from the dead before the church submitted to Him (Rom. 5:8). He had to serve like crazy before submission was earned (Mark 10:45).

Jesus didn't demand submission before He served. He served thoroughly, and then opened the opportunity for people to submit to Him. This is why He said to Peter, "If you don't let me wash you, you have no part with me." Jesus had served, but if Peter couldn't submit himself to receive Jesus' service, then they couldn't walk together.

Leaders must serve first—this creates a healthy and safe place for people to submit to them. But if people choose not to receive their service, then there is no submission, and they cannot walk together. If a leader isn't serving, then there is nothing to submit to. *Submission is allowing yourself to receive the service of a leader.*

IN CONCLUSION

Ultimately, when the healthy fivefold is fully operating, there will be no more false religions such as Islam, Buddhism, Hinduism, Judaism, New Age, or Atheism. All will bow their knee to the good King

Jesus. False teachers and teachings will be silenced. Spiritual infants will become fully matured sons. Everyone will be adjusted into their place in the body. Each member of the body will take ownership of their metron and function with their grace. We are heading toward all things on the planet being like heaven. The future is bright!

> *He made known to us the mystery of his will according to his good pleasure, which he purposed in Christ, to be put into effect when the times reach their fulfillment—**to bring unity to all things in heaven and on earth under Christ**. (Eph. 1:9-10).*

CHAPTER TEN

IMPLEMENTING THE KINGDOM MODEL

We have covered a lot of material in this book so far, and this is the chapter where the practical application comes into play. It is a challenge to lay out a practical plan for the local assembly, considering that some churches are home-group based, and some meet in stadiums. When church membership ranges from 10 people to 1 million people, church structure can be very different. I don't believe that church leadership structures are holy or anointed. Leaders have been given the same fivefold graces and callings since the early church, but the structures of local churches have been—and continue to be—vastly different.

When people in the early church gathered, they met in each other's houses. They didn't build church buildings, because they were under persecution from the Jerusalem temple leaders until AD 70. After the destruction of the temple, Christians began to convert whole regions, growing so large that they even began to meet in the existing pagan temples.

I specifically remember touring the ruins of Laodicea when I visited Turkey in 2015. I saw a temple that formerly belonged to Zeus worshippers, which had been converted into a Christian church in the first century. I mention this because many modern Christians seem to think that home groups are the magic structure for New Testament Christianity. This idolization of home groups considers the Roman Emperor Constantine to be the bad guy who wrongly moved the church into church buildings in the 300s.

Just as local church structure should not become an idol, neither should church leadership structure. We want to recognize and work with the graces that God has given, while also allowing flexibility for their structure and format.

Let us begin by looking at the "official" structure of the church. Then we will distinguish between the global and local church, and end by laying out practical advice for putting the fivefold into practice in a local church.

OFFICIAL POSITIONS

In this book, we have focused primarily on the fivefold graces and their metrons. It is now time to look more closely at the idea of "official offices" in the New Testament. An "office" is conferred by the laying on of hands by:

- An apostle (Acts 6:6, 14:23, 1 Tim. 5:22, 2 Tim. 1:6, Titus 1:5)
- A body of elders (Acts 13:1-3, 1 Tim. 4:14)

An office is something that your character must qualify you for (Acts 6:3-6, 1 Tim. 3, Titus 1:5-9) and which your character can disqualify you from continuing in (1 Tim. 3:6-7, 5:19-20).

There are three types of positional-authority "offices" conferred by the laying on of hands in the New Testament:

- Apostles (Acts 1:20, Acts 13:1-3, 1 Tim. 4:14)
- Elders (1 Tim. 3:1)
- Deacons (Acts 6:6, 1 Tim. 3:8)

These three "offices" are unique from the other four of the fivefold in Ephesians 4:11 (prophet, evangelist, pastor, and teacher), and they are also unique from the gifts of the Holy Spirit listed in 1 Cor. 12:4-11.

Sometimes overlap exists where the elders and deacons are comprised of the other four (prophet, evangelist, pastor, and teacher) of the fivefold. Here are two examples:

1. Philip was a deacon (Acts 6:5) and an evangelist (Acts 21:8)
2. The Ephesian leaders were elders (Acts 20:17) and shepherds (i.e. Pastors, Acts 20:28).

The New Testament record is not clear enough to make a definitive statement such as, "All elders should be fivefold leaders." It seems that there could be elders and deacons who qualify as leaders of the local assembly based on character, but who may not have fivefold grace on their life. Conversely, perhaps there were fivefold-graced people that were not elders in the local assembly.

UNIVERSAL VS. LOCAL CHURCH

Now, let's look more closely at the office of the apostle in the universal church and the local church.

Jesus mentions the "church" twice in the Gospels (Mt. 16:18, 18:17). In Matthew 16:18, He says to Peter regarding the revelation that Jesus is the Messiah: *". . . on this rock I will build my church, and the gates of Hades will not overcome it."* Here, Jesus is speaking of the universal church—the spiritual, global church.

Then in Matthew 18:15-17, Jesus says:

> *"If your brother or sister sins, go and point out their fault, just between the two of you. If they listen to you, you have won them over. But if they will not listen, take one or two others along, so that 'every matter may be established by the testimony of two or three witnesses.' If they still refuse to listen, tell it to the church; and if they refuse to listen even to the church, treat them as you would a pagan or a tax collector."*

In this passage, Jesus is not saying to go tell the global/spiritual/universal church. He is speaking of the church as a local assembly, the church in the local context.

The elders and deacons are appointed to care for the needs of the local church assembly (1 Tim. 5:17). In contrast, the apostles are "sent ones." They are sent out from the local assembly for the good of the global/spiritual/universal church (1 Cor. 10:32).

When we are confused about this division of focus—apostles/global, elders-deacons/local—we can easily read passages such as Ephesians 2:20, which speak of the church being built on the foundation of the apostles and prophets, and think that every local church must have their own apostle. This causes a feeling of lack, which usually leads to rebranding the local senior pastor as an apostle. One of the biggest problems with that is that the senior pastor has no influence outside of the local church, so he isn't serving the global/spiritual church, and he hasn't become a "sent one" because he is still sitting in the same church doing almost exactly the same work he has done for decades. This actually waters down our ability to recognize the role of truly functioning, "sent" apostles.

If we could simply see that Ephesians 2:20 is saying that the global church is built on the foundation of the apostles and prophets, rather than the local assembly being built on the apostles and prophets, we could avoid a host of confusing problems.

With that said, I do see that all the local assemblies in the New Testament had relationship with an apostle (Paul, Peter, James, Barnabas, Apollos). And some of the apostles themselves were both elders in the local church as well as "sent ones" for the good of the global church (see 1 Peter 5:1).

I believe that every local church assembly needs relationship with at least one apostle who gives input and participates in the ordination of elders and deacons. I do not believe that they need "covering" or to be in the apostle's "downline." The apostle belongs to the global church and comes to wash the feet of the local leadership.

To state my point clearly: Apostles occupy an office in the global church. They think and focus globally. They are constantly looking out for the wellbeing of leaders and raising up new elders, deacons, and fivefold-graced leaders.

The offices of elders and deacons are given to the local church; they think and focus locally. They are constantly looking at the wellbeing of their local congregation, protecting, strengthening, and increasing the flock.

SHIFTING TO A FIVEFOLD CHURCH

I will now offer advice on the general process for moving toward a fivefold-influenced church.

The first hurdle will be the title of "pastor." In the modern

Protestant church, whoever is the senior leader of a local church is the "pastor." Even if they don't have an ounce of pastor grace on their life, it is the *de facto* title.

If we can mentally step back from that title and remember what an actual shepherd/pastor is and looks like, we will likely find that there are individuals currently on staff who are counseling, bringing healing to marriages and families, making hospital visits, officiating at weddings and funerals, and bringing community and fellowship into the local church through home groups, picnics, etc. *These* are the individuals with the pastor grace on their life.

Maybe your senior leader truly has a pastor grace, but maybe not. Teachers or prophets are often leading churches under the title of "pastors," simply because of our modern church culture. Step one: We must stop mislabeling people (especially the senior leader).

Next, we must not rush to throw titles on people. If we are careless about rapidly giving out titles, we will actually hinder the progress toward having a fivefold-influenced church. Even Paul told Timothy not to rush when putting people into leadership positions (1 Tim. 5:22).

We must also take time with our leadership team to become acquainted with the fivefold graces and how they function. There are a few ways that this can happen—books, trainings, summits, and academy mentorships.

I can't say I agree with everything in the following books, but they lay a good foundation for any leadership team to start with:

The Complete Wineskin by Harold R. Eberle

Fivefold Ministry Made Practical by Ron Myer

Apostles Today by C. Peter Wagner

Apostles Today by Benjamin Scott

I also suggest finding events led by each of the fivefold graces and sending your leaders to them. For example: send your prophets to an event or training session led by a prophet.

The Welton Academy provides a mentorship program for fivefold leaders, and we are at your service to help raise up your leaders. Welton Academy Summits are hosted by our fivefold team, and these are great events to equip your leadership.

Next, I suggest bringing in guest speakers to your church who are strong in the fivefold graces. This will expose your congregation to the five different flavors of grace.[22]

Begin to publicly acknowledge the graces that are on the individuals in leadership at your church. Do not be shy about the grace that God has given to leaders in your assembly. Honor releases value, and valuing a grace increases the flow of that grace.

Create opportunities and platforms for the other graces to influence the assembly. For example, you could set aside funding for the evangelist to buy sleeping bags for the homeless in your city, and take teams out to give them away and minister. Another example would be having an evening service twice a month for the prophet to do supernatural services with an emphasis on healing, prophecy, etc.

It is important for those leaders who are being acknowledged as developing into a fivefold grace to have time to gather and connect

---

[22] A mental picture that I personally find helpful is to think of the fivefold as five different oils, each with a different color and scent. For example:

The prophet is dipped in purple oil (lavender).

The evangelist is dipped in red oil (cinnamon).

The pastor is dipped in yellow oil (lemon).

The Teacher is dipped in green oil (peppermint).

The graces are very distinct. And what of the apostle you might ask? The apostle typically begins by being dipped in one of the other graces for a season, and then they get dipped a second time with the apostle grace, which then blends with the first grace they were dipped in. Therefore an apostle-prophet is very distinct from an apostle-teacher or an apostle-evangelist, etc.

with the other fivefold graces in the church. The graces should not be isolated into spending time only with graces of the same type. The best-case scenario is when the five graces can cross-pollinate and receive influence from each other while recognizing their uniqueness.

There should come a time where each matured fivefold leader on the team should be announced and acknowledged publicly in front of the congregation. This should be fasted and prayed about with the team beforehand and should include a public laying-on of hands where more grace will be imparted. A service dedicated to this can be very worthwhile, and having an apostle present that the team is in relationship with can greatly increase confidence and impartation during such a service. This gives the congregation a better ability to draw on the grace on that leader's life (Matt. 10:41).

It is important that the fivefold team in a local church keep the focus on the fact that they are graced together with the purpose of washing the feet of the local congregation. Each of the graces needs the others to operate for the church to be fully equipped and healthy.

Remember that "equip" means to adjust a bone. The evangelist needs the pastor to adjust the bones of the people he evangelizes— they need their lives healed and made whole. The pastor needs the teacher to adjust his people so that they are not blown around by every wind of doctrine but are rooted and grounded in truth and freedom. The teacher needs the prophet to shake up his people so that they do not become theoretical, but are alive to the invisible world. We are all working together for the benefit of the local body and we need each other. There is no room for power struggles or comparing one with another.

SO, WHO LEADS?

No one particular grace should always be at the head of a local church. You can tell who the leader is by asking, "Who has the largest sphere of influence in the local assembly?"

Is it the pastor who visits everyone and builds a strong sense of family and community? Does everyone look to this person as the senior leader of the church? (Typically, pastors lead churches between 1-99 people.)

Is it the impassioned evangelist who is regularly preaching on the streets and doing outreach programs and altar calls? Does everyone look to this person to as the senior leader of the church? (Typically, evangelists lead "seeker-sensitive" churches; these churches often have thousands of people but lack deeper teaching.)

Is it the profound teacher who is regularly doing in-depth teaching series and classes? Does everyone look to this person to as the senior leader of the church? (Present-day teachers are typically found in ministry schools and seminaries, or teaching an adult Sunday school or mid-week class. Yet, in the 1800s, many churches were led by teachers, and Sunday morning services were three or more hours long and contained deep theological teaching.)

Is it the prophet who ushers the congregation into awareness of the spiritual realm and an encounter with God? Does everyone look to this person as the senior leader of the church? (Typically, when a prophet leads a church, everyone in that church is trained to prophesy, pray for healing, pray for impartation, etc. Normally these churches are less than 100 people and very unstructured and free-flowing.)

Is it the apostle who is constantly giving a worldwide perspective to the local congregation? Because apostles are "sent ones," they typically are not the long-term[23] leaders of a local congregation. In the time they lead a local congregation, lots of fivefold leaders will be raised up and empowered, the local congregation will think in global terms regarding kingdom advancement, and other churches will be reaching out to pull on the apostolic grace on that local leader. The

---

[23] Paul was in Corinth for 18 months (Acts 18:11) and Ephesus for 3 years (Acts 20:31), but essentially he kept on the move for his larger metron.

church that is heavily influenced by an apostle will be a model to other congregations, such as Paul said of the Thessalonians:

> *"You became imitators of us and of the Lord, for you welcomed the message in the midst of severe suffering with the joy given by the Holy Spirit. And so **you became a model to all** the believers in Macedonia and Achaia. The Lord's message rang out from you not only in Macedonia and Achaia—your faith in God has become known everywhere."* (1 Thess. 1:6-8)

Whichever senior leader has the biggest sphere/metron of influence in the local congregation will be the one who needs to find, recognize, and stir up the other graces so that they balance out what is missing and bring all the grace of Christ into effect in the local church.

THE IDEAL

Each fivefold leader needs a platform to influence people within the local church. The ideal that I long to see would have the teacher dynamically speaking on Sunday morning in the public service, the pastor focusing on the health of families and marriages in the congregation, the prophet having supernatural services one evening per week as well as classes in the supernatural, and the evangelist taking people outside the church to do outreach, ministry to the poor, missions trips, etc. A local church led by these four graces would be a very healthy, balanced church, and these four leaders would also be in relationship with an apostle—in many cases outside their local church—who would travel and visit as a father or mother while staying in touch when not in town. In some cases, the local church may be the sending base of an apostle, such as Antioch was the sending base of Paul. But when Paul was needed locally to stand up to Peter, he was present for his local church (Gal. 2:11).

The prophet, evangelist, pastor, and teacher work as a team and as the plurality of elders in a local church. Not all four need to be paid, fulltime staff of the church. Every situation is different. It would be amazing to have finances set up in such a way that the teacher can pour his heart into study and teaching prep, the pastor can counsel, lead home groups, and bring great health to the church, the evangelist can take teams out continuously to reach the community, and the prophet can train the whole church in the supernatural and maintain a deep prayer life with fasting and speaking in tongues daily. If we can balance the finances in a way that balanced the priorities of the different graces, we can have a very well-rounded church.

The goal of an apostle is to get the local churches in his metron functioning in a manner similar to what has been described. Many have taken on the title of apostle and continued to act identical to the "pastoral" model of a one-man show. In contrast, true apostles will establish a team of people representing all the graces and will build them to work together as one unit, representing all the graces of Christ in a local body. As wise master builders, apostles will provide guidance, direction, and the architecture of the local church development.

CONCLUSION

*T*he green military jeep pulled up in front of an army tent. This time, when the general entered the tent, only one officer was present, and he snapped to attention.

"At ease," said the general.

The officer dropped his salute and the general asked, "You are the teacher, correct? Where are the other officers?"

"Yes, sir. I am preparing my teachings. The other officers are out at their posts."

Nodding, the general said, "I've heard good reports from this station."

"Thank you, sir. Since you sent your team and equipped us, our officers have been trained in their specific tasks. We have also promoted other soldiers within our ranks when we discovered their giftings. The change in company morale is massive."

The general smiled, "Not to mention, the casualty rate has dropped off dramatically."

The teacher smiled as well. "Permission to speak frankly, sir?"

"Granted."

"On behalf of my fellow officers, thank you for equipping us. You taught us to properly equip others and better lead within our regiments. Because of that, we now fight more strategically, and we've been able to send the enemy into full retreat."

The general said, "That is my pleasure and my duty."

He lifted his hand in salute, and the teacher did the same.

In unison, they said, "For the kingdom."

PRACTICAL QUESTIONS ABOUT FIVEFOLD MINISTRY

I've heard many questions about the fivefold. Most of them have been addressed in this book, but since there were more, I am including this resource Q&A to provide a few more tools for the equipping process.

What should I do if my leadership does not believe in my gifting/ calling?

If you operate in the grace on your life—say evangelism—it becomes undeniable over time. Many people have put the cart before the horse. If they simply prophesied and encouraged people to learn how to hear God's voice, then the recognition of their calling as a prophet would follow. Unfortunately, many people try to get the recognition first.

What practical means of training should I undergo for my fivefold calling?

- Study everything the Bible says about your fivefold grace.
- Read every other book on the topic that you can.
- Go to training events about your fivefold grace.
- Find others who are recognized in that grace and follow their model.
- Also, I would highly recommend attending Welton Academy Online.

Should I be set/ordained in my fivefold calling?

Eventually, every fivefold grace should be publicly recognized with the laying on of hands. This is a time when your metron expands and greater grace is imparted.

What should the leadership of a local church do if they realize their congregation is "under-equipped" in one or several of the five areas because nobody in their church seems to operate in that grace?

It is more likely that the congregation includes individuals with the fivefold calling, but they are lying dormant. The best thing to do would be to bring in guest speakers who are recognized in the missing grace. This will awaken those in the congregation with that calling. Then those local leaders can be developed.

Can two individuals carry the same fivefold grace even though one of them has a metron of ten people and the other a metron of ten thousand? And can you give practical examples of what this would look like?

Yes. The apostles Paul, Peter, and Apollos each had differently sized metrons. And whereas Paul ministered to the Gentile world, Peter ministered to the Jewish world (Gal 2:7-8).

Could an individual operate in one fivefold grace while they are in one geographical area or with a certain group of people and then switch to a completely different grace when they are in another area?

Yes. This is based on the dynamics of how people are receiving and pulling grace from you. In one region, you may be received as a prophet, so the people receive the prophet's reward, yet in another region you may be received as a teacher, so the people receive the teacher's reward (Matt. 10:41).

One challenge with this variance is when people try to pull on a fivefold grace that you do not have. For example, I can be pulled on for apostle-teacher, and sometimes as prophet, but if I am being pulled on as an evangelist or pastor, I have no fivefold grace to give in those arenas. You cannot pull out a grace that a person is not carrying.

WOMEN IN LEADERSHIP[24]

M any years before the time of King David, Israel was enslaved by the Canaanites. The Israelites had once again walked away from the Lord and—as happened so many times during that era— they were enslaved again. Deborah the prophetess was the recognized national leader among the Hebrews during that time.

The Lord directed Deborah to bring Israel out of slavery. Deborah prophesied to a man named Barak that he was to gather a volunteer army of ten thousand men to fight for freedom. She also provided his battle strategy and assured him of victory. Barak realized he was being given a tremendous honor with this prophetic word. Although he may have been tempted to keep the honor of this victory for himself and the men of the army, he chose instead to honor Deborah in return:

> *Barak said to her, "If you go with me, I will go; but if you don't go with me, I won't go." "Very well," Deborah said. "I will go with*

[24] A version of this section previously appeared in my book *Normal Christianity* (Destiny Image, 2011).

you. But because of the way you are going about this, the honor will not be yours, for the LORD will hand Sisera [the enemy general] over to a woman . . . " (Judges 4:8-9)

Barak had no obligation to honor Deborah. He could have kept the honor for himself and his men, but he chose to share the honor with Deborah. By doing so, he passed the honor to all women. Deborah did not keep the honor to herself; she went on to declare that Barak would not get the honor, and neither would she, but rather the honor would go to an unnamed woman. In the divine exchange between Deborah and Barak, we see a divine order of empowerment between the genders.

Presently, the church is full of wonderful Deborahs who have been honoring men for many years. It is time for a company of Baraks to rise up—humble and confident men who are not willing to keep the honor of leadership to themselves, men who will empower women to step into their call and destiny.

Many have been asking the Lord, "Where are the Deborahs?" but a better prayer would be, "Lord, raise up men as a Barak company!"

WHERE IT ALL BEGAN

From the very beginning of humanity there has always been a battle for dominance between the sexes. Let us go back and see where it all started:

Now the serpent was more crafty than any of the wild animals the LORD God had made. He said to the woman, "Did God really say, 'You must not eat from any tree in the garden'?" The woman said to the serpent, "We may eat fruit from the trees in the garden, but God did say, 'You must not eat fruit from the tree that is in the middle of the garden, and you must not touch it, or you will die.'" "You will not surely die," the serpent said to the woman. "For God knows that when you eat of it your eyes will be opened, and you will be like God, knowing good and evil."

When the woman saw that the fruit of the tree was good for food and pleasing to the eye, and also desirable for gaining wisdom, she took some and ate it. She also gave some to her husband, who was with her, and he ate it. Then the eyes of both of them were opened, and they realized they were naked; so they sewed fig leaves together and made coverings for themselves.

Then the man and his wife heard the sound of the LORD God as He was walking in the garden in the cool of the day, and they hid from the LORD God among the trees of the garden. But the LORD God called to the man, "Where are you?" He answered, "I heard You in the garden, and I was afraid because I was naked; so I hid." And He said, "Who told you that you were naked? Have you eaten from the tree that I commanded you not to eat from?" The man said, "The woman You put here with me—she gave me some fruit from the tree, and I ate it." Then the LORD God said to the woman, "What is this you have done?" The woman said, "The serpent deceived me, and I ate." (Gen. 3:1-13)

After this, God placed a curse upon the serpent, a curse upon the woman, and a curse upon the ground that Adam would be tending. The curse placed upon the woman is the curse that caused the gender war. What was this curse?

To the woman He said, *"I will greatly increase your pains in childbearing; with pain you will give birth to children.* **Your desire will be for your husband, and he will rule over you"** (Genesis 3:16).

This phrasing works as a statement of action and reaction. Because the woman "desires" her husband, he will "rule over" her. Yet this does not make much sense as a curse. Why should a woman's desire for her husband cause him to dominate her? Most men would gladly accept their wife's desires for them, causing them to treat her more gently rather than roughly, as is implied in this verse. So how are we to understand this?

The key is in the word "desire," translated from the Hebrew *tesuqah*, which occurs only three times in the Old Testament. It is best understood through its usage in Genesis 4:7, which shows another side, that of a desire to overcome or defeat another: "[Sin's] *desire is for you, but you should rule over it.*"

Thus, God is saying that a woman's desire will be to gain the upper hand over her husband, but because she is the weaker vessel, her husband will put her down by force, if need be. The curse is essentially that women will lose the battle of the sexes. History bears this out. Until the advent of women's rights movements, women were virtually their husband's property, treated as heir-producing machines, given little freedom, and forced to serve their husband's every whim. In many cultures, men bought and sold women like cattle. Some cultures maintain this custom even today. In fact, women's rights have only existed in mainstream Western culture since Susan B. Anthony and the Suffrage Movement of the 1920s.[1]

ADAM NAMES THE WOMAN

After God had released the curses for rebellion, including the subjugation of woman, Adam named his wife. Until this point in the story (see Gen. 1-3:19), his wife was only referred to as *the woman*, but now Adam doles out a name for her. And so, *the woman* becomes *Eve*. This may seem small and insignificant, but if we consider that Adam and *the woman* had walked as equals before the curse, this is actually a profound detail: *"Adam named his wife Eve, because she would become the mother of all the living"* (Gen. 3:20).

Previously, Adam had been given dominion in Genesis 1:28 to

rule over all the animals, birds, and fish, but he did not rule over woman until the curse occurred. When the woman received the curse of subjugation, Adam named her in the same manner that he had named all the animals of the garden (see Gen. 2:19-20). By naming *the woman*, Adam took dominion over *Eve* in the same way that he took dominion over the animals. And so the curse was applied and enacted. God called this a curse because He never desired for them to be unequal. It was not God's intention, but rather a result of sin. In fact, in the story of Noah, we find that God worked to bring restoration of equality in the Old Testament.

NOAH AND HIS SONS

By the time we get to Genesis 6:5-7, we find that the earth had become wicked. We learn of God's plan to wipe out the first creation with a worldwide flood and start again with the only righteous people on earth: Noah and his family. Skipping ahead in the story, God had Noah build an ark in preparation for the flood:

> **And Noah and his sons** and **his wife and his sons' wives** entered the ark to escape the waters of the flood. (Gen. 7:7)

> On that very day **Noah and his sons**, Shem, Ham and Japheth, together with **his wife and the wives of his three sons**, entered the ark. (Gen. 7:13)

Sometimes it can seem like the Bible provides us with odd details, but it is surprising how much can be contained in small statements. Looking at these two verses you can see that Noah and the other men went into the ark first, and then the women followed. Once the flood was over, God gave Noah very specific directions as to how to exit the ark.

> *Then God said to Noah, "Come out of the ark, **you and your wife** and **your sons and their wives**"* (Gen. 8:15-16)

God intended to bring the eight of them out of the ark as couples walking in unity and equality. He was trying to start the planet over with at least a partial redemption of gender equality. Unfortunately, we read that Noah disobeyed the Lord's specific instructions: *"So Noah came out, together with his sons and his wife and his sons' wives"* (Gen. 8:18). We see from this that God desired to restore women, but man's disobedience got in the way. Not much progression in the restoration of equality took place between the garden of Eden and when Jesus came upon the scene 4,000 years later. As we will see, though, what Jesus accomplished changed everything.

JESUS, THE ULTIMATE REDEEMER

In the garden of Eden, there was equality between men and women. In heaven, there will be no curses (see Rev. 22:3), which means that women will be fully restored. Currently, we live in a timeline between these two curseless realities: the garden of Eden and heaven. When Jesus entered this timeline where men and women live on earth under the curses, He came to bring us freedom. Jesus came to bring the future reality of heaven into our present. He even passed this commission to His church when He told us to bring heaven (future) into earth (present):

> *This, then, is how you should pray, "Our Father in heaven, hallowed be Your name, Your kingdom come, **Your will be done on earth as it is in heaven**"* (Matt. 6:9-10)

Because of what Jesus accomplished on the cross—freeing humanity from the power of the curse—we do not have to wait until heaven for the curse to be removed. In fact, according to Paul, Jesus has changed the current timeline so that we do not dwell under gender, economic, or racial curses any longer:

You are all sons of God through faith in Christ Jesus, for all of you who were baptized into Christ have clothed yourselves with Christ. There is neither Jew nor Greek, slave nor free, male nor female, for you are all one in Christ Jesus. (Gal. 3:26-28)

Jesus came to redeem all humanity from every curse, including the curses incurred by Adam and Eve in Genesis 3. Because we have been placed inside of Christ and Christ has been placed inside of us, it doesn't matter whether we are a Jew, slave, female, or Greek—all in Christ are equal. If we were able to see this from the perspective of God the Father when He looks at individuals in His church, we would see that He is not looking at male and female, African or European, bank owner or welfare recipient—He is looking at the heart and seeing Christ.

This is what God was trying to explain to the prophet Samuel when he was searching for the next king of Israel: *"Man looks at the outward appearance, but the LORD looks at the heart"* (1 Sam. 16:7b).

The Lord's perspective is different from ours. Consider that God has never been under any curse; therefore, He does not treat us according to the curses. The Genesis 3 curse never said that women were going to be accursed of God and therefore could not be used for leadership. The curse only changed the way that men and women would interact, not the way that God would interact with women.

God has always looked not at the outward appearance, but at the heart of the believer, which is where Jesus is dwelling. So when God looks at a believer, it does not matter to Him whether the believer is male or female, because He is looking at the Christ in that person. Paul was urging the Galatians to see each other in this same way.

The Genesis 3 curse never changed God's interaction with women, and Jesus' redemption was to change our interaction with each other.

We, as ambassadors of heaven, as those seated in heavenly places, are to bring heaven's reality into this world. One aspect of bringing that reality into this realm is bringing equality back to our sisters, mothers, daughters, and wives.

NAME RECOGNITION

Before we look at some of the amazing women of God who were listed as fellow ministers alongside the apostle Paul, we need to understand the power of name recognition. Author Bob Sorge gives incredible insight into this topic:

> The desire for the praise and approval of man runs very deep in our sinful flesh. We can crucify the desire for man's praise, but it keeps resurfacing in our flesh in all kinds of creative and fresh ways.
>
> Paul was aware of the insidious trap that young men fall into, for they can easily convince themselves that their motives are totally pure in seeking the praise of God alone, when in fact this desire for the praise of man is still a very strong issue within them. Paul showed his sensitivity to this issue in the way he related to one brother in the book of Second Corinthians.
>
> Here the context of the matter to which I refer:
>
> *I thank God, who put into the heart of Titus the same concern I have for you. For Titus not only welcomed our appeal, but he is coming to you with much enthusiasm and on his own initiative. And we are sending along with him **the brother** who is praised by*

all the churches for his service to the gospel. What is more, he was chosen by the churches to accompany us as we carry the offering, which we administer in order to honor the Lord himself and to show our eagerness to help. We want to avoid any criticism of the way we administer this liberal gift. For we are taking pains to do what is right, not only in the eyes of the Lord but also in the eyes of men.

*In addition, we are sending with them **our brother** who has often proved to us in many ways that he is zealous, and now even more so because of his great confidence in you. As for Titus, he is my partner and fellow worker among you; as for our brothers, they are representatives of the churches and an honor to Christ.* 2 Corinthians 8:16-23

Paul is writing about two brothers—Titus and an unnamed brother. Titus is mentioned twice by name and commended; the other brother is left nameless. Why does Paul not mention the other brother's name? Because Paul knew the power of name recognition.

There's something intoxicating about seeing your name in print and having your name known by others. I've tasted of that wine personally just a little bit; Paul also knew all about that. And he was aware that the brother to whom he was referring didn't have the maturity to handle the fame properly. So Paul refused to make his name known. There's no doubt in my mind that the unnamed brother was young, new in ministry, and still in training. Titus, on the other hand, was safe to name because of his evident maturity and proven faithfulness.

We might think this was an accidental oversight on Paul's part until we realize that he repeated the same thing the second time in the same epistle. The following verse comes four chapters later:

> *I urged Titus to go to you and I sent **our brother** with him. Titus did not exploit you, did he? Did we not act in the same spirit and follow the same course?* 2 Corinthians 12:18

For the second time, Paul mentions Titus twice by name while leaving his companion nameless.[2]

Now let us apply this profound insight about name recognition to the topic of women in leadership. Keep in mind that the apostle Paul, who avoided mentioning the name of Titus's traveling companion, did not hesitate to commend many female ministers in his writings.

PAUL'S CO-LABORERS

In Romans 16, Paul points out many women by name without hesitation. This speaks volumes about the level of their character and leadership in the early church. For example, the chapter starts by acknowledging a female deacon named Phoebe:

> *I commend to you our sister **Phoebe, a deaconess** of the church in Cenchrea. I ask you to receive her in the Lord in a way worthy of the saints and to give her any help she may need from you, for she has been a great help to many people, including me.* (Rom. 16:1-2)

Then Paul acknowledges Priscilla and Aquila in verses 3 and 4. Look closely, and you will see that he makes a statement that wouldn't even be proper in modern times. Paul put the wife's name first. Even in modern etiquette this is considered taboo. Etiquette states that we address a couple as Mr. and Mrs. Jonathan and Karen Welton. It would be considered improper and poor taste to address a couple as Karen and Jonathan Welton. Yet, the apostle has no qualms about acknowledging Pricilla first and her husband second:

Greet Priscilla and Aquila, my fellow workers in Christ Jesus.
They risked their lives for me. Not only I but all the churches of the
Gentiles are grateful to them. (Rom. 16:3-4)

Paul continues and acknowledges Mary (who served in ministry),
Tryphena, Tryphosa, and Persis:

*Greet **Mary**, who worked very hard for you.* (Rom. 16:6)

*Greet **Tryphena and Tryphosa**, those women who work hard in*
*the Lord. Greet my dear friend **Persis**, another woman who has*
worked very hard in the Lord (Rom. 16:12)

Considering the caution Paul used when it came to name recognition,
it is a powerful statement that he named so many female co-workers
in Romans 16. It is unfortunate that Paul has been given such a
bad reputation of supposedly suppressing women. I believe that the
church has largely misunderstood much of what Paul actually wrote
regarding women. I will show you later in this section how some of
these misunderstandings have occurred.

FEMALE APOSTLES AND PROPHETS

By examining Romans 16, we can see that Paul was very much in
favor of women in ministry, but we have not yet looked at high
positions of authority given to women in Scripture, so let's continue
our investigation:

*And in the church God has appointed **first of all apostles, second***
***prophets**, third teachers, then workers of miracles, also those*
having gifts of healing, those able to help others, those with gifts of

administration, and those speaking in different kinds of tongues.
(1 Cor. 12:28)

We understand from this passage that apostles are the highest position of authority in the church. In fact, Ephesians 2:20 tells us that the apostles and prophets are the foundation of the church. Therefore, if a woman could be an apostle or a prophet, wouldn't it stand to reason that she could be placed in lower positions of authority such as evangelist, teacher, or pastor? I believe that stands to reason!

There are four women listed as prophetesses in the Bible, three in the Old Testament and one in the New Testament. (Note: The title "prophetess" has no less authority than the male equivalent "prophet," because they come from the same root word.)

The first is Miriam: *"Then Miriam the prophetess, Aaron's sister, took a tambourine in her hand, and all the women followed her, with tambourines and dancing"* (Ex. 15:20).

The second is Deborah, who was not only a prophetess but was the leader of Israel: *"Deborah, a prophetess, the wife of Lappidoth, was leading Israel at that time"* (Judges 4:4).

The third is Huldah the prophetess: *"Hilkiah the priest…went to speak to the prophetess Huldah…"* (2 Kings 22:14).

The fourth is our New Testament example, Anna: *"There was also a prophetess, Anna, the daughter of Phanuel, of the tribe of Asher. She was very old; she had lived with her husband seven years after her marriage"* (Luke 2:36).

From these four examples we can see that God has no problem having a woman as a prophet, the second highest level of authority in the church. If a woman can be a prophet, then she can be a lower position like a senior pastor, right?

But what about an apostle? Is there any evidence of a female apostle in the New Testament? Yes! There is a clear example of a female apostle in the New Testament. In fact, she and her husband are both listed together as apostles—and not just ordinary apostles. They are called *"outstanding among the apostles"*:

> *Greet Andronicus and Junias, my relatives who have been in prison with me. They are outstanding among the apostles, and they were in Christ before I was.* (Rom. 16:7)

There is no scholarly rebuttal to the fact that Junias was a first century female name. In fact, the name Junias is a derivative of the name Juno, the Roman goddess and wife of Jupiter. As the patroness of marriage, Juno was sought after for the dilation of the cervix for safe child delivery. Junias was without question a female name, so this passage of Scripture is proof of a female apostle.

Many Christians argue over what position a woman can hold in ministry. Some will allow a woman to teach children, some will let them teach the youth group, some will say she can hold administrative roles, and sometimes maybe she can be an assistant pastor, but typically the role of senior pastor is out of the question. However, the concept that a female cannot be in the sacred position of senior pastor is biblically hard to defend. If you examine the word *pastor* in Scripture, you will find a major flaw in the argument. The word *pastor* is only used once in all of the New Testament (Eph. 4:11), as I noted earlier in this book. Even in this one reference, there is no definition or instruction as to who can and cannot be a pastor. Yet culturally we have created definitions that restrict women from access to the most vague of all New Testament leadership gifts.

We have seen that women can reside in the highest places of authority in the church as apostles and prophets. Therefore, they rightfully can hold any of the lower gifts or callings throughout the church. However, many churches have banned women from these positions because of three passages in the New Testament. Let us investigate these highly debated verses.

THE TROUBLE VERSES

Case #1: 1 Peter 3:6-7

The late Bible teacher Kenneth E. Hagin has a great insight into this verse and its application. Here is what he has to say about 1 Peter 3:6-7:

> Peter cites Sarah as a model wife whose worthy example Christian wives could follow.
>
> They were **submissive** to their own husbands, like Sarah, who obeyed Abraham and called him her master. You are her daughters if you do what is right and do not give way to fear. 1 Peter 3:5b-6
>
> It is possible to lift this one verse out and say, *"See, the wife is to obey her husband just as Sarah obeyed Abraham."* But does it mean the wife doesn't have any right to speak her own mind? Some would leave the impression the wife never has a right to express her thoughts, that she's under the rule—the obedience—the domination—and is nothing more than a slave. But that isn't what Peter is saying. Let's see what the law says:

Then Sarai said to Abram, "You are responsible for the wrong I am suffering. I put my servant in your arms, and now that she knows she is pregnant, she despises me. May the LORD judge between you and me." "Your servant is in your hands," Abram said. "Do with her whatever you think best." Then Sarai mistreated Hagar; so she fled from her. - Genesis 16:5, 6

Here we see Abram letting Sarai have her own way. He isn't dominating her like some warlord. From the 16th chapter of Genesis through the 21st there is an account of a disagreement. At its climax, we see that Abraham gave in to his wife's contention, and let her have her own way. And we see that God justified not him, but her.

"And she said to Abraham, "Get rid of that slave woman and her son, for that slave woman's son will never share in the inheritance with my son Isaac." The matter distressed Abraham greatly because it concerned his son. But God said to him, "Do not be so distressed about the boy and your maidservant. Listen to whatever Sarah tells you, because it is through Isaac that your offspring will be reckoned." - Genesis 21:10-12

God told Abraham, one time at least, to listen to his wife. According to this, Sarah ruled her husband on this occasion. And God approved of it, as He always does when a wife is right."[3]

There has also been a tendency in the church to view women as unqualified for places of high leadership because they are considered the "weaker vessel." This comes from a misapplication of 1 Peter 3:7:

Husbands, in the same way be considerate as you live with your wives, and treat them with respect as the weaker partner ["weaker vessel" KJV] *and as heirs with you of the gracious gift of life, so that nothing will hinder your prayers.*

First of all, Peter is speaking here about the husband and wife relationship. Notice how he starts by saying, *"Husbands."* Second, he tells the husband three things about how to treat his wife: *"be considerate," "with respect,"* and *"as heirs with you."* He even gives an ominous warning about how the husband's prayers could be hindered if he doesn't get this right. Then he uses the phrase *"weaker partner"* in the middle of the passage. In this case, the King James Version brings more clarity, rendering that phrase as *"weaker vessel."* The word "vessel" refers to dishware, as in a plate or a bowl. So to say that a wife is a weaker bowl or plate is essentially to say that a wife is to be treated like *fine china.*

Fine china is not your typical dinnerware that you throw in the dishwasher and then into the cupboard. No, it requires a gentleness that carefully washes it by hand, and it is usually displayed in a glass-front china cabinet where all can admire it. "Women are fine china and should be treated with respect, gentleness, and considerateness" is the correct understanding of the phrase "weaker vessel."

Case #2: 1 Timothy 2:11-14

> *A woman should learn in quietness and full submission. I do not permit a woman to teach or to have authority over a man; she must be silent. For Adam was formed first, then Eve. And Adam was not the one deceived; it was the woman who was deceived and became a sinner.* (1 Tim. 2:11-14)

Without understanding the correct context, it is easy to see how these verses are used to oppress women. In any careful study of the letters of Paul, one must first answer the following questions: To whom is the letter written? What is it regarding? Is this directive applicable to every person, everywhere, for all time?

When verses of the Bible are quoted out of context, they can easily be misused. For example, we must understand that Paul was speaking in hyperbole and frustration when he said, *"As for those agitators, I wish they would go the whole way and emasculate themselves!"* (Gal. 5:12). If we do not understand these verses in their proper context, it would be easy to create a eunuch cult. This is no exaggeration; over the years many thousands of people have participated in suicide cults based on slight mis-teachings of the Bible. It is desperately important that we look closely at what we believe and why.

There is an important saying: *Right teaching leads to right living.* It would make sense that the opposite is also true: *Wrong teaching leads to wrong living.* Wrong teaching about women in leadership has led the church to the mistreatment of women for hundreds of years.

Let's look at those questions we should ask of this text:

Question #1: To whom was the letter written?

1 Timothy is a letter from the apostle Paul to his spiritual son Timothy, who at that point was recognized as an apostle in Ephesus. A close look at the following passages reveals the problems in Ephesus. Here is what Paul was writing to Timothy about:

Have nothing to do with godless myths and old wives' tales; rather, train yourself to be godly. (1 Tim. 4:7)

Besides, they get into the habit of being idle and going about from house to house. And not only do they become idlers, but also gossips and busybodies, saying things they ought not to. (1 Tim. 5:13)

Question #2: What is it regarding?

From these verses as well as the historical evidence, we learn that one of the major problems in the Ephesian church was women going from house to house spreading evil teachings and doctrines of demons (see 1 Tim. 4:1). We are informed in chapter 1 that the reason for writing to Timothy was to correct this issue. Some translations say to *"command certain men not to teach,"* but the roots of this verse show that it was a gender-neutral statement: *"command certain persons not to teach."* This is important because it was actually women who were teaching erroneous doctrines in Ephesus. Paul wanted them silenced—not because of gender, but because of heresy:

> *As I urged you when I went into Macedonia, stay there in Ephesus so that you may command* **certain persons** *not to teach false doctrines any longer or to devote themselves to myths and endless genealogies. Such things promote controversial speculations rather than advancing God's work—which is by faith.* (1 Tim. 1:3-4 TNIV)

As we have seen, the issue was not certain men, but more accurately, certain women. Today's New International Version has done a great job translating in this case, because the non-gender-specific Greek pronoun *tisi* is used here.

Question #3: Is this directive applicable to every person, everywhere, for all time?

This personal letter between Paul and Timothy is not broadly applicable to all churches everywhere. Some of it is personal, contextual advice. Paul had left Timothy in charge of the church in Ephesus, and Timothy had to straighten out the false teachings of the local women. We must apply the words of Paul in a little less personal and a little more contextual manner.

For example, Paul told Timothy to stir up the gift that was in him from when Paul laid hands upon him. Obviously, you and I have not had the apostle Paul lay hands on us for impartation of spiritual gifts, but that does not mean that we can disregard this verse. We must treat this verse in context as something we can still learn from. We learn from this that spiritual gifts can be imparted by the laying on of hands and that they need to be stirred up within us as well. Scripture must be kept inside its correct context.

Author J. Lee Grady gives insight into the situation that Timothy was dealing with in Ephesus:

> Bible scholars have documented the fact that bizarre Gnostic heresies were circulating throughout the region at that time, and these false teachings posed a serious threat to the infant Christian churches that were budding in that part of the world. That's why so much of Paul's message to Timothy deals with how to guard against false teaching.
>
> This teaching most certainly bred unhealthy attitudes among some women in the Ephesian church. These women were completely unlearned, but they were spreading false doctrines, and in some cases they were claiming to be teachers of the law and demanding an audience. They were most likely mixing Christian and Jewish teachings with strange heresies and warped versions of Bible stories. Some even taught that Eve was created before Adam and that she "liberated" the world when she listened to the serpent.[4]

"For Adam was formed first, then Eve. And Adam was not the one deceived; it was the woman who was deceived and became a sinner" (1 Tim. 2:11-14). What Mr. Grady has written explains why Paul would write such a seemingly out-of-place statement. The culture at that time was saturated with false teachings about what took place in the garden of Eden, who was created first, and who was deceived. Ephesus at the time was the seat of the fertility goddess Diana (see

Acts 19), and the new believers who were getting saved out of the occult were young in the Lord and very confused by their past. Paul was teaching Timothy how to manage his situation as the leader. The direction from Paul is a very specific and unusual context, which should not be applied to everyone, everywhere, for all time.

To gain more insight into what was really going on in Ephesus, we need to look closely at the phrase *"to have authority over."* The root word used for authority in the verse is *authentein*, and it is used only one time in the New Testament: *"I do not permit a woman to teach or **to have authority** over a man; she must be silent"* (1 Tim. 2:12). The Greek word that is typically used for authority in the New Testament is *exousia*.

Bible scholars have noted that *authentein* has a forceful and extremely negative connotation. It implies a more specific meaning than "to have authority over" and can be translated "to dominate," "to usurp," or "to take control." Often when this word was used in ancient Greek literature, it was associated with violence or even murder. A clearer picture of what Paul told Timothy is that he doesn't allow a woman to violently steal authority. But are we to think that Paul would allow a man to violently steal authority just because he is a man? Obviously, the issue was not gender. In reference to this specific problem, Paul was instructing Timothy not to allow these women who were trying to take control and usurp authority.

In Paul's letter to Titus, Paul addressed a similar problem. In this case, it was men who were causing the problem:

> *For there are many rebellious **men**, empty talkers and deceivers, especially those of the circumcision, **who must be silenced** because they are upsetting whole families, teaching things **they should not teach** for the sake of sordid gain.* (Titus 1:10-11 NASB)

The fact that this verse has never been used to tell all men everywhere that they must be silent and cannot teach is indicative of the one-sided approach that the church has taken toward women.

LETTER STRUCTURE

One last thought on this passage is that the chapter divisions inside the letters of Paul are not divinely inspired; they are simply a manmade construct to make reading easier. Yet at times they cause more problems than they help. For example, 1 Timothy is divided into five chapters, and the reading breaks seem quite arbitrary. If an individual were to read straight through 1 Timothy without chapters and verses, they would notice that this letter is much more naturally divided into four major sections:

1. Introduction: 1 Timothy 1:1-14
2. "Here is a trustworthy saying that deserves full acceptance": 1 Timothy 1:15
3. "Here is a trustworthy saying": 1 Timothy 3:1
4. "This is a trustworthy saying that deserves full acceptance": 1 Timothy 4:9

These three "trustworthy" sayings of Paul are the focus of his letter to Timothy. After Paul states each saying, he then expands on the thought presented and how it applies to Timothy's leadership.

To see the context of 1 Timothy 2:11-15, we must back up to 1 Timothy 1:15 and look at the first trustworthy saying:

Christ Jesus came into the world to save sinners – of whom I am the worst. But for that very reason I was shown mercy so that in me, the worst of sinners, Christ Jesus might display his immense patience as an example for those who would believe in him and receive eternal life. Now to the King eternal, immortal, invisible, the only God, be honor and glory forever and ever. Amen.

Then, from 1 Timothy 1:18-2:15, Paul expands upon this saying and gives very practical instruction:

- 1 Timothy 1:18-20 Paul admonishes Timothy specifically
- 1 Timothy 2:1-7 Paul admonishes the whole church
- 1 Timothy 2:8 Paul admonishes men
- 1 Timothy 2:9-10 Paul admonishes women (plural)
- 1 Timothy 2:11-14 Paul admonishes about a specific woman (singular)
- 1 Timothy 2:15 Paul admonishes women (plural)

Because we have not seen the context, 1 Timothy 2:11-14 and verse 15 have been tremendously confusing. Here it is in the NIV:

*A **woman** [singular] should learn in quietness and full submission. I do not permit **a woman** [singular] to teach or to assume authority over a man; **she** [singular] must be quiet. For Adam was formed first, then Eve. And Adam was not the one deceived; it was the woman who was deceived and became a sinner. But **women** [plural] will be saved through childbearing— if they continue in faith, love and holiness with propriety.*

According to the original manuscripts, Paul goes from writing in the plural about all women in 2:9-10, to writing in the singular, in reference to a specific woman who was causing problems in the Ephesian church. Paul is instructing Timothy specifically about what was going on in the Ephesian church and how to handle this trouble-making woman.

Then there is the bizarre and mysterious verse 15: *"But women will be saved through childbearing."* Fortunately, I have not to heard an altar call for women to get pregnant so they can earn their salvation. Nonetheless, there is a lot of confusion and oppression that has happened with this verse. The problem is created by an error in translation. Here is the same verse in the Young's Literal Translation: *"she shall be saved through **the** childbearing."*

That little *"the"* makes a huge difference.

In context, Paul was just writing about Adam and Eve (1 Tim. 2:13-14). Back in Genesis 3:15, God speaks of the offspring of Eve crushing the head of the serpent, which we understand is a prophecy of Jesus' defeat of the devil at the cross.

Therefore, Paul is not saying women who give birth will be saved; he is saying that women are saved through "The Child" that was born in fulfillment of Genesis 3:15, which is Jesus! This brings us full circle to the trustworthy statement about the message of salvation, which Paul started with in 1 Timothy 1:15-17.

Case #3: 1 Corinthians 14:34-35

As in all the congregations of the saints, women should remain silent in the churches. They are not allowed to speak, but must be in submission, as the Law says. If they want to inquire about something, they should ask their own husbands at home; for it is disgraceful for a woman to speak in the church. (1 Cor. 14:34-35)

In our previous "trouble verse," we looked at the situational context and how the words from Paul to Timothy do not apply to everyone, everywhere, for all time. Yet when we look at this last and most troubling of the three trouble verses, it seems to be the harshest.

Regarding subjugation of women it states the following:

- This rule applies to all congregations (everyone, everywhere, for all time).

- They must be silent in church.

- They are not allowed to speak.

- No asking questions.

- It is disgraceful for a woman to speak in church.

We must understand that 1 Corinthians is a response letter to *the Corinthians*. They wrote to Paul, and he wrote back: *"Now for the matters you wrote about..."* (1 Cor. 7:1). This puts the situation into context.

As one would with any response letter, Paul at times quotes from the Corinthians' original letter to put his response into context. We are not able to see this in our modern English versions, but by looking closely at the original Greek, we can see that certain parts of 1 Corinthians were not written by Paul but were quotes from their first letter to him. This is key to explaining 1 Corinthians 14:34-35.

In the Greek, it is evident that 1 Corinthians 14:34-35 is a quote from the original letter to Paul (See endnote #5). If Paul taught that it is disgraceful for a woman to even speak in church, then why would he spend time teaching that women should have their heads covered when prophesying in church (see 1 Cor. 11:2-16)? Prophesying is more than speaking; it is speaking *for* God, so if it is a shame for a woman to speak, wouldn't it be worse to claim that she is speaking for God?

If we step back from just focusing on 1 Corinthians 14:34-35 and look at the verses before and after, we will see the dialogue that is taking place between Paul and the Corinthians:

What then shall we say, brothers? When you come together, everyone has a hymn, or a word of instruction, a revelation, a tongue or an interpretation. All of these must be done for the strengthening of the church. If anyone speaks in a tongue, two— or at the most three—should speak, one at a time, and someone must interpret. If there is no interpreter, the speaker should keep quiet in the church and speak to himself and God.

Two or three prophets should speak, and the others should weigh carefully what is said. And if a revelation comes to someone who is sitting down, the first speaker should stop. For you can all prophesy in turn so that everyone may be instructed and encouraged. The spirits of prophets are subject to the control of prophets. For God is not a God of disorder but of peace. (1 Cor. 14:26-33)

As in all the congregations of the saints, women should remain silent in the churches. They are not allowed to speak, but must be in submission, as the Law says. If they want to inquire about something, they should ask their own husbands at home; for it is disgraceful for a woman to speak in the church. (1 Cor. 14:34-35) [This is the quoted portion.]

Did the word of God originate with you? Or are you the only people it has reached? If anybody thinks he is a prophet or spiritually gifted, let him acknowledge that what I am writing to you is the Lord's command. If he ignores this, he himself will be ignored. Therefore, my brothers, be eager to prophesy, and do not forbid speaking in tongues. But everything should be done in a fitting and orderly way. (1 Cor. 14:36-40)

In verses 26-33, Paul is teaching how a church service should be so that everyone can participate, then in verses 34-35 he quotes from the Corinthians' letter to him regarding their philosophy of how to run a service. Paul immediately responds in verses 36-40 with a very harsh rebuke to the Corinthian leaders. Apparently, he strongly disagreed with their thoughts expressed in verses 34-35.

There is a sensible flow to Paul's response when we see the quoted section in the middle. Paul even uses the same language in both of his statements, *"For God is not a God of disorder but of peace . . . everything should be done in a fitting and orderly way"* (1 Cor. 14:33, 40). And of course, Paul is not contradicting what he said earlier about how a woman should prophesy in church.

It is easy to see how the common misunderstandings in these three passages have led Christian leaders to keep women from leadership. Please understand that most Christian leaders are just trying to follow the Word to the best of their understanding. If they have not been shown the errors in these teachings, then they are taking these verses at face value and trying to be obedient without malicious intention.

CONCLUSION

For hundreds of years, women have been oppressed and suppressed by male chauvinistic church leadership. The terrible misconception is that the Bible is sexist. Unfortunately, when the Bible is read with only a surface understanding, it appears to say some negative things about women. The reality is that the Bible strongly speaks of freedom and equality between the genders. I am hopeful that after reading this chapter and taking this closer look, many lives will have new freedom, deeper healing, and restoration between genders.

Endnotes:

[1] Richard T. Ritenbaugh http://bibletools.org/index.cfm/fuseaction/Bible.show/bibleBook/1/sChap/3/sVerse/3/sVerseID/72/eVerseID/72/opt/comm/RTD/cgg/version/kjv; accessed February 11, 2011.

[2] Bob Sorge, *Dealing with the Rejection and Praise of Man* (Lee's Summit, MO: Oasis House, 1999), 39-40.

[3] Kenneth E. Hagin, *The Woman Question* (Tulsa, OK: Rhema Bible Church, 1983), 16-17.

[4] J. Lee Grady, *10 Lies the Church Tells Women: How the Bible has been misused to keep women in spiritual bondage* (Lake Mary, FL: Charisma House, 2000), 57.

[5] Gilbert Bilezikian, Th.D. *Beyond Sex Roles: What the Bible Says About a Woman's Place in Church and Family.* 2nd ed. (Grand Rapids: Baker Book House, 1985). ISBN: 0-8010-0885-9. On page 248, Bilezikian writes:

> It is worth noting that in 1 Corinthians more than in any of his other Epistles, Paul uses the é particle to introduce rebuttals to statements preceding it. As a conjunction, é appears in Paul's Epistles in a variety of uses. But the list below points to a predilection for a particular use of é, which is characteristic mainly of 1 Corinthians.

The verses he listed I also list below, in the order they appear, with a notation indicating the appearance of the é particle, in each case translating it as "Nonsense!" as Bilezikian did to indicate its flavor: 1 Cor. 6:1-2—"If any of you has a dispute with another, dare he take it before the ungodly for judgment instead of before the saints? (é Nonsense!) Do you not know that the saints will judge the world? And if you are to judge the world, are you not competent to judge trivial cases?

The é of which he speaks is the Greek letter *"eta,"* which looks like **h**. This device is called the "rhetorical *eta*." Many of my Greek professors confirmed its use. Paul uses this device many times in 1 Corinthians. Its importance here is that it clearly marks a refutation of the previous passage. That is what the rhetorical *eta* is for—it indicates that what precedes it immediately is being refuted. Since the Greeks did not have quotation marks, this device serves as quotation marks and shows the injunction against women speaking was actually the statement of the Corinthians to Paul. Apparently some faction in the church, perhaps Judaizers, or some group the Corinthians has been in contact with, had said this to them.

We can see this clearly in English, if we know what to look for.

The verse states: (35)"If there is anything they desire to know, let them ask their husbands at home. For it is shameful for a woman to speak in church."

(36) **What!** Did the word of God originate with you, **or** are you the only ones it has reached?"

Clearly that sounds like a reversal of what has been said. One can get a sense of the refutation of the previous remark, after all, those who want to allow women to speak are not demanding that men be silent. Why would they seem to come across as thinking that they were the only ones to hear from God? That idea makes much more sense if they wanted to silence someone. It makes more sense in speaking to the silencers, because they are acting like they are the only ones to receive the word of God.

Those italicized words "what" and "or" represent where the h comes. There are two of them, grammatically two of them should make it say "what, or" but they can also function as rhetorical and that fits the sense of the passage much better. Otherwise it sounds like nonsense, with Paul railing against those he supports! So the *etas* are here: "**h** Did the word of God come only to you? **h** Are you the only ones it has reached?" This signals the refutation of the previous idea, the silencing of women.

WELTON ACADEMY

The Welton Academy Supernatural Bible School Online is neither a supernatural ministry school nor a dusty seminary. We have created a unique program that teaches the depths of the Word without becoming boring or denying the supernatural. We are focused on teaching the Bible through a new covenant kingdom perspective.

It is our passion to see all Christians operate in the supernatural, know their identity, walk in freedom, and be powerful people. We are not simply aiming at creating pastors and missionaries. No matter what your calling is, you must have a firm foundation in your identity, freedom, and the supernatural. We think long-term and build powerful people.

To be a part of where the Lord is leading the church in the years to come, we must lay a new foundation in our understanding of the Word. The Word hasn't changed, but some of our understanding of it must change; otherwise, we will hinder our growth and the advancement of the kingdom of God.

A powerful advantage of the SBS is that while you are spiritually growing you are not isolated. You have the opportunity to interact with others who are growing in the same deep things you are learning. You are joining a movement with others who are pressing forward with God.

Go to www.weltonacademy.com for registration and more information.

RAPTURELESS
Third Edition

In 2012, the best-selling author and founder of Welton Academy, after ten years of thorough research, released the first edition of *Raptureless*. It has gone viral and has sent a shockwave through the Charismatic/Pentecostal church world. Dr. Welton's writing gift has made *Raptureless* one of the easiest to read yet deepest quality books on the subject of the endtimes. He proves beyond a shadow of a doubt that the Great Tribulation is an event, which occurred in the first century. Without complicated wording, he demonstrates that the Antichrist is not a person in our future, and that we are not waiting for Jesus to be enthroned in Jerusalem. Basically, this book is the opposite of everything you thought you knew about the end times, simply written and thoroughly, historically proven. Now available in it's third edition, with new editing and chapter reordering, as well as 60% more content than the original.

What others have said:

"Jonathan Welton has taken a bold step in confronting one of the greatest 'sacred cows' of our day: end time theology! The fear created by the expectation of a coming antichrist and a great tribulation are keeping many believers in bondage. Many believe that defeat is the future destiny of the Church. In his easy-to-read presentation, Jonathan dismantles many of the popular ideas in the Church about the end times." ~ Joe McIntyre

Additional Material by Dr. Jonathan Welton

UNDERSTANDING THE WHOLE BIBLE
The King, The Kingdom, and the New Covenant

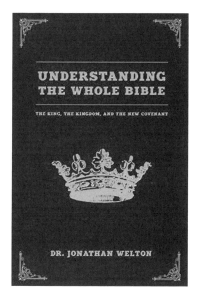

This textbook is the distillation of a nineteen-week course, "Understanding the Whole Bible from Genesis to Revelation" taught by author and theologian Dr. Jonathan Welton. If you want to devour the Word, this textbook will give you the knife and fork, and even tuck in your napkin and teach you how to eat! Topics include: - Learn the difference between Systematic and Biblical Theology - How did we get our Bible? - Translations and study tools - Free will versus Predestination - Dispensationalism and Covenant Theology - Cessationism and Supernaturalism - The Five Major Covenants: Noah, Abraham, Moses, David, and the New Covenant - The Covenant Promises fulfilled - God is not an Old Covenant monster - Understanding the At-One-Ment - Better Covenant Theology - The Great Covenant Transition - The End of Age - The Unveiling of Jesus - The One Law of the New Covenant World.

What others have said:

This is an instant classic. 'A book that shows the Bible is the story of God's covenant journey with His people.' Dr. Jonathan Welton has presented one of the most comprehensive and revelatory books on the King, the Kingdom, and the New Covenant.

Jonathan Welton has shifted my entire understanding of the Bible and his book provides so much clarity on what the Bible really is saying. Seeing Scripture through the lens of the covenants is so needed and many miss this vital perspective.

Understanding the Seven Churches of Revelation

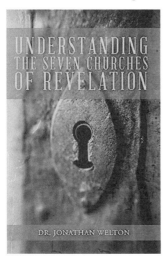

What little has been written about the seven letters to the churches in Revelation tends to utilize the lens of interpretation called dispensationalism. But the book itself gives us no indication that the letters to the churches are anything but letters to churches in the first century. In this unique book, Jonathan Welton applies the historical-contextual method of hermeneutics to these letters, which begins with the questions *who, where, when, what,* and *why.*

Jonathan delves deeply into the historical context of each individual letter for excellent, but often hidden insight. Since church history tells is that each of these churches was a literal historical church (not a metaphor, as dispensationalism proposes) John was addressing specific situations relevant to each church during the first century. When we look at the historical and cultural dynamics of the cities, we find that the letters are, in fact, very specific and unique to the historic reality.

Says the author:

"I have read other historically thorough sources, and I have done my own research, including traveling to and touring the modern locations of each of the seven churches mentioned in chapters 2 and 3 of the book of Revelation. In doing so, I have discovered an incredible list of connections between the cultural, geographical and historical events of the first century in these cities and the contents of Jesus' letters to them. I've written the book I wish I had read when I was seventeen and eager to understand what these beautiful yet cryptic letters were all about. I believe these letters hold significant and relevant information that influences our understanding of this book as a whole and that holds practical relevance for our lives."

New Age Masquerade

By far this is the most unique book regarding the New Age Movement from a Christian perspective. Jonathan Welton reveals the history of the New Age Movement from Swedenborgism to the modern New Age, while demonstrating that each of the movements leaders originally had roots within Christianity. The New Age isn't a Christian movement, but it is a movement away from a Christian foundation.

Other Topics covered:
- What is the difference between a Christian and a New Ager?
- Are we to have showdowns like Elijah vs the Prophets of Baal?
- How do we discern the counterfeit from the authentic?

Are you curious about what the Bible says about: The Age of Aquarius, the silver cord, necromancy, the Zodiac, ESP, Automatic writing, ectoplasm, and zombies? This book is for you!

From the Foreword by Patricia King

"Jonathan Welton has done a tremendous job writing *New Age Masquerade*. In it, he brilliantly discloses the biblical foundations that have been counterfeited in specific New Age practices. The enemy has take Scriptural truth, twisted it, and dangled it before the spiritually hungry. He knows all people were created for encounter with God, and his goal is to draw people away from Jesus and unto himself.

"Remember, if there is a counterfeit, there must be an authentic. In *New Age Masquerade*, Jonathan will introduce you to the authentic."

The School of the Seers by Jonathan Welton

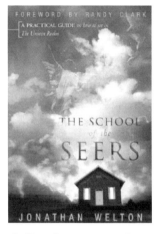

Your how-to guide into the spirit realm!

The School of the Seers is more than a compilation of anecdotal stories. It is the how-to guide for seeing into the spirit realm.

The fresh, profound, and new concepts taught in this book take a mystical subject (seers and the spirit realm) and make them relevant for everyday life.This book takes some of the difficult material presented in other seer books and makes it easy to understand, removes the spookiness, and provides practical application of a dimension that is biblically based and scripturally sound. Get ready to enter the world of a seer! In this groundbreaking and revelatory book, Jonathan Welton describes his unique journey in which God opened his spiritual eyes. He shares how you too can activate this gift in your life.

Discover the keys from Scripture that will help you:

- See with your spiritual eyes.
- Use the four keys to greater experiences.
- Recognize what may be hindering your discernment.
- Learn about the four spirits.
- Access divine secrets and steward heavenly revelation.
- Learn how to really worship in Spirit and in Truth.
- Understand meditation, impartation, and so much more...

Normal Christianity: If Jesus is Normal, what is the Church? by Jonathan Welton

Jesus and the Book of Acts are the standard of *Normal Christianity.*

Remember the fad a few years ago when people wore bracelets reminding them, What Would Jesus Do? Christians state that Jesus is the example of how to live, yet this has been limited in many cases to how we view our moral character. When Christians tell me they want to live like Jesus, I like to ask if they have multiplied food, healed the sick, walked on water, raised the dead, paid their taxes with fish money, calmed storms, and so forth. I typically receive bewildered looks, but that is what it is like to live like Jesus!

Perhaps we are ignoring a large portion of what living like Jesus really includes. Many Christians believe they can live like Jesus without ever operating in the supernatural. After reading in the Bible about all the miracles He performed, does that sound right to you? (Excerpt from book)

What others have said

I believe before Jesus returns there will be two churches. One will be religious, and the other will be normal. This book of Jonathan Welton's will help restore your childlike faith, and you will become normal!

~ **Sid Roth,** Host of It's Supernatural! Television Program

ADDITIONAL MATERIAL BY JONATHAN WELTON
Eyes of Honor: Training for Purity and Righteousness
by Jonathan Welton

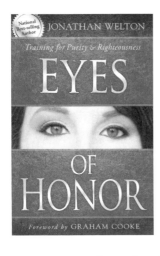

After struggling with sexual temptation for years, author Jonathan Welton devoted himself to finding a way to be completely free from sexual sin. He read books, attended 12-step groups, and participated in counseling—with no success.

Spurred on by countless friends and acquaintances who shared a similar broken struggle and longed for freedom, the author searched Scripture. There he found the answer, which he shares with you in a compassionate, nonjudgmental way.

Eyes of Honor helps you understand how to live a life of purity by realizing:

- Your personal identity
- How to view the opposite sex correctly
- Who your enemies are

Eyes of Honor is honest and refreshing, offering hope and complete freedom and deliverance from sexual sin. Jesus' sacrifice on the cross and your salvation guarantee rescue from the appetite of sin. Your true identity empowers you to stop agreeing with lies of the enemy that ensnare you.

"This book is stunningly profound. He got my attention and kept it." **~ Dr. John Roddam**, St. Luke's Episcopal

"Jonathan has written one of the best books on being free from bondage by dealing with the root issues of sin. I highly recommend reading this book.

~ Dr. Che Ahn, Chancellor Wagner Leadership